DANGEROUS DAYS
IN
ANCIENT
EGYPT

By the same author

Dangerous Days in the Roman Empire

Dangerous Days on the Victorian Railways

Dangerous Days in Elizabethan England

DANGEROUS DAYS
IN
ANCIENT
EGYPT

*A history of the terrors and the torments,
the dirt, diseases and deaths
suffered by our ancestors*

Terry Deary

WEIDENFELD & NICOLSON

First published in Great Britain in 2015
by Weidenfeld & Nicolson

1 3 5 7 9 10 8 6 4 2

© Terry Deary 2015

A CIP catalogue record for this book
is available from the British Library.

HB ISBN-13 978 0 297 87062 3

Printed and bound by CPI Group
(UK) Ltd, Croydon, CR0 4YY

The Orion Publishing Group Ltd
Carmelite House
50 Victoria Embankment
London, EC4Y 0DZ

An Hachette UK Company
www.orionbooks.co.uk

The Orion Publishing Group's policy is to use papers
that are natural, renewable and recyclable products and made
from wood grown in sustainable forests. The logging and
manufacturing processes are expected to conform to the
environmental regulations of the country of origin.

For Oliver Burdess

CONTENTS

INTRODUCTION

> 'Marley was dead, to begin with. There is no doubt whatever about that.'
>
> *Charles Dickens (1812–70), opening of* A Christmas Carol

Ancient Egypt. Dead, all dead. Not just dead but dead for 5,000 years. Other eras are remembered for what they did when they were alive.

🪲 The Normans? Crusaded and crushed.

🪲 The Tudors? Sailed and swashbuckled.

🪲 The Victorians? Engineered and empire-built.

But the Ancient Egyptians are remembered for what they did *after* they died.

🪲 The Egyptians? Mummies and pyramids, sarcophagi and statues.

> 'Two vast and trunkless legs of stone
> Stand in the desert. Near them, on the sand,
> Half sunk, a shattered visage lies …
> Nothing beside remains. Round the decay
> Of that colossal wreck, boundless and bare
> The lone and level sands stretch far away.'
>
> *Percy Bysshe Shelley (1792–1822), English poet: 'Ozymandias'*

Awesome, eh? But Ozymandias and his statue weren't fictions from Shelley's fevered brain. Old Oz is known today as Ramesses II.* His 'shattered visage' had been unearthed by Italian archaeologist and grave-pillager Giovanni Battista Belzoni. The Italian adventurer transported it to the British Museum, irreparably damaging historic Egyptian buildings as he struggled to get the sculpture out. It was the imminent arrival of Ozymandias's head in London that inspired Percy Bysshe's poem.

But all is not what it seems. It rarely is in poetry … or history. Shelley's fantasy says a traveller described how 'Two vast and trunkless legs of stone / Stand in the desert', which is such a powerful image of the mighty fallen, hollow pretentions and illusory power. Death conquers all, etc.† But Oz's statue was a bust, not a long-legged statue.

Then Percy Bysshe says that on the pedestal this classic line from the stony lips of King Oz appears …

---

* Ramesses II has had his mummy examined and it appears his face suffered blackheads. These are not depicted on the statue that stares down at you in the British Museum. Airbrushing of celebrity images is not confined to the computer age.

† Or 'Mors vincit omnia' if you want to impress your friends with the Latin take on mortality. Usually best said after several pints of beer when the company has reached the morbid-drunk stage.

> 'Look on my works, ye Mighty, and despair!'

While we wallow in the wisdom and wonder at the wit of Bysshe, we forget to ask the crucial, clinical question: 'Hang on … how could you, Percy, know what was on the pedestal when it would be another 30 years before Egyptian writing could be deciphered?' By the time Ramesses' words were translated, Percy Bysshe would have been long-drowned off the coast of Italy and cremated on the beach. Still, his poem about Ozymandias became a posthumous popular success and Britain was becoming interested in the antiquities of Ancient Egypt.

In the Victorian era Thomas Pettigrew (1791–1865) achieved fame for his private parties at which he unwrapped and dissected mummies for the pleasure of his guests. The idea came from a meeting he had with Giovanni Battista Belzoni.

The Italian had enlisted the doctor's help in examining the shrivelled corpses. Pettigrew had little idea how much his cadaver-cutting would fascinate the world. The mummy-mangling displays were so magical they were over-subscribed. One cold January evening in 1834 an unwrapping was witnessed by a prince, bishops, statesmen and MPs, doctors, artists and authors. It was standing-room only. The Archbishop of Canterbury and the Bishop of London tried to gain admittance (by hook or by crooks), but failed – bet they were cross.

The Duke of Hamilton was so awed by Thomas Pettigrew's work that he hired the doctor to mummify *him* after his death.* The Duke died in August 1852, and Pettigrew obliged.

---

* Why? A man who *destroys* mummies is employed to *create* one? Does that make sense to you? Would you go to a scrap-yard dismantler to build your next car?

The mummy unwrappers were the sensation of the day and parodied in poetry ...

> 'On Friday evening they stripped a corse –
> A mummy they called it – and what was worse,
> Sawed through the head – as if it were cheese
> (Praise be where due, it made them sneeze),
> Then placed upon its feet the insulated dead,
> Gave three wild yells – then went to bed.'
>
> Punch *Magazine*

Fifty years later, in 1908, Egyptologist Margaret Murray was unrolling one of the 'insulated dead' for 300 morbid men and woman to spectate. It took place in the Chemistry Theatre at Manchester University (which gave the ghoulish display a touch of academic respectability). Egyptomania had lift-off.

> 'Khnumu Nekht was bared of his wrappings and brought once more to the light of day. Near the body the linen sheets had rotted, and they fell to pieces at a touch. The bones, however, were more or less perfect. There were traces of flesh on them. It was on the whole a gruesome business, and one or two people left early.'*
>
> Manchester Guardian, *7 May 1908*

---

* It was only considered worthy of report because it was a woman doing the unwrapping for the first time. Mummies had been the objects of public curiosity since the 1500s. A hundred years after the first European find, Charles II gathered the dust from Egyptian mummies and rubbed it into his body. He believed that some of their greatness would rub off onto him.

Then in 1922 came the booster rocket that sent Egyptophilia*
into orbit. The discovery and display of the forgotten young
king Tutankhamun. It wasn't mere morbid fascination this
time, it was the glitter of gold that drew the public to wade
through the dusty silences of the museums to witness the
funerary objects. There was the frisson of the 'Curse of the
Mummy' too.

Everyone wanted a piece of the Egypt glamour. Movies
were made with moving mummies to awe the audiences.
Egypt became a tourist destination as Europe flocked to look
at stones and sand – as if Blackpool didn't have enough.

The 'colossal wrecks' like the statue of Ramesses II, the
pyramids, the Valley of the Kings – and remnants like the
mummies – are such moving monuments to Death that it's
easy to forget the makers were once alive.

> 'History is the depository of great actions, the witness
> of what is past, the example and instructor of the
> present, and monitor to the future.'
> *Miguel de Cervantes (1547–1616), Spanish author*

The Ancient Egyptians lived and loved, plotted and played,
feared and fought and fretted as humans always have and
probably always will. But every age experiences its own
dangers.

The lives of Ancient Egyptians are still obscured by the
bandages of time. But we can try unwrapping those lives to
see what their tombs can tell us. Ye shall know them by their
deaths.

---

* Oh, all right, I made up that word. I think.

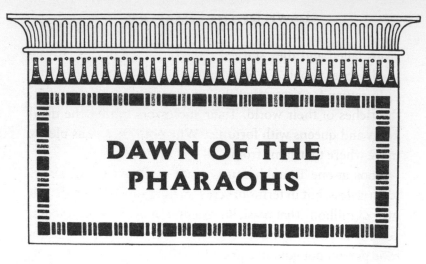

DAWN OF THE PHARAOHS

DYNASTIES 0 TO 2
THE EARLY DYNASTIC PERIOD
(3150–2686 BC)

> 'The only wealth which you will keep forever is the
> wealth you have given away.'
>
> *Marcus Aurelius (AD 121–180), Roman emperor*

The palaces of history have often been populated by
crooks. But in Ancient Egypt it really was a crook. A
shepherd's crook was the symbol the pharaohs chose to show
they were shepherds of their people. Caring pharaohs.

The other symbol was a flail for corn and that was a
promise they would feed their people. Did the Egyptian
peasants fall for this propaganda? Probably not when their

crops failed and they starved. (Of course a flail can also be used to beat people – it was dangerous to cross the king.)

In return for protecting the people, the pharaohs held all the riches of their world. Their successors buried the dead kings and queens with fortunes. Why not? There was plenty more where that came from.

Look at one Tutankhamun's death mask. As a work of art it's priceless, but in terms of scrap-metal value it is worth well over £1 million. That mask has become an icon of the ancient land. It is also a symbol of twisted thinking. Why would a sane person put gold in a grave?

'Why would a king go to his tomb with treasures?' you ask.

The ancients answer: 'So that the king can keep his status in the next life.'

A depressing thought. Heaven is a pleasure palace for the rich? Sounds more like Hell.

> 'You can't take it with you, and even if you did, it would probably melt.'
>
> *Dorothy Parker (1893–1967), American poet and satirist*

Sounds like the world today.

Meanwhile, back in the world of Ancient Egypt, the poor starved for want of the gold underground. Those poor set out to rob the graves … and who can blame them?

> 'Probably the greatest harm done by vast wealth is the harm that we of moderate means do ourselves when we let the vices of envy and hatred enter deep into our own natures.'
>
> *Theodore Roosevelt (1858–1919), 26th US president*

Who were these crook-carrying kings with a craving for cash-rich coffins? Glad you asked ...

— FASCINATING PHARAOHS* —

> 'Denial ain't just a river in Egypt.'
>
> *Mark Twain (1835–1910), American author and humorist*[†]

> 'For Man to tell how human life began is hard; for who himself beginning knew?'
>
> *John Milton (1608–74) English poet:* Paradise Lost

In the beginning was the Nile. The rich soil alongside it was known as 'The Black Land'. Then there was the desert – 'The Red Land'. The hunter-gatherers arrived at the Nile and stopped hunter-gathering. They settled there in tribes. But you know how it is. Someone takes charge. A chief.

He (it's usually a 'he') assimilates other tribes and before you know it you have a culture. That assimilation could well have been violent. A smack on the head with a prehistoric club is a universal language meaning, 'I am now in charge here.' In Egypt these tribes grew and spread and merged till there were just two along the Nile – north and south. But ...

---

* Pharaoh doesn't literally mean 'king'. It means 'Great House' in ancient Egyptian. The rulers were too great to be called by their actual name. Naming a leader after their residence is like calling the US president Mr Whitehouse or the King of France Mr Versailles, or the Russian leader Mr Kremlin. They're fine names. But, in the UK, Mrs Buckingham-Palace is not quite so euphonious.

† Some say this is misattributed to Twain. But it's the sort of thing he may have said, so let's give him the credit.

Pharaoh fallacies

> 'And he swam and swam up the river until all he could see before him was a large bottle of tomato ketchup. It was the sauce of the Nile.'
>
> BBC radio programme I'm Sorry I'll Read That Again *(1973)*

There are conspiracy theories that say the little tribes *never* united to form big ones. According to the theorists, the pharaohs came from outside Egypt and imposed themselves on the tribes with their superior intelligence. The 'proof' is the pharaohs' skulls were longer – with more brain capacity – than the typical Nile-side peasant.

This theory is deeply racist and sprang from one of the most eminent and talented archaeologists, Flinders Petrie (1853–1942).

> 'If the name of any one man must be associated with modern excavation as that of the chief begetter of its principles and methods, it must be the name of Professor Sir W.M. Flinders Petrie.'
>
> *James Baikie (1866–1931), Egyptologist*

Flinders Petrie was known as 'the father of pots' and his work transformed the world of archaeology. Sadly, like so many world-changing pioneers, he was a flawed human. And Petrie's flaw was his devotion to the idea of 'eugenics'. He was a racist who was convinced by the theory of white supremacy.

Did you know ... eugenics

Eugenics is about improving the human race by making sure people with desired traits (positive eugenics) reproduce like rabbits while those with undesired traits (negative eugenics) do not.

How do you stop the negatives from reproducing? Castrate the men or remove the ovaries of the women. A quicker way is to simply exterminate the 'negatives'. Genocide. How do you decide what the 'positive' human qualities may be? Ah, that's the question.

The eugenics idea was devised by Charles Darwin's half-cousin Francis Galton (1822–1911). His theories were welcomed by many in the early 20th century and ultimately adopted by Adolf Hitler and his Nazi followers. Millions died for Galton's theory.

Petrie's banal principles affected his work. Fellow Egyptologist Wallis Budge proposed quite reasonably that the Egyptians were East Africans. Petrie's prejudices wouldn't countenance that. The Egyptians were a superior people (he argued) and white-skinned Northern Europeans are a superior people, therefore the Egyptians were invaders. They conquered the 'inferior' natives of Africa.

If the Northern Europeans were so superior, how come they didn't build mighty structures in their homelands? By 2400 BC that astonishing engineering feat, the Great Pyramid, had been standing for 200 years. What did Europe have? A pile of children's building blocks called Stonehenge.

Flinders Petrie lived long enough to witness the Nazis put his eugenic theories into genocidal practice yet never shifted in his beliefs. Sad.

If you want a *really* wacky theory then the 'outsiders' came from outside planet Earth – they were aliens. You can write the rest yourself, can't you? 'Ah, yes,' you nod wisely. 'That explains how they could create those massive pyramids in a prehistoric age. Anti-gravity lifting devices – operated from their flying saucers.'

Why stop there? Those pyramids, some learned writers have declaimed, are actually arranged as beacons for the intergalactic spacecraft to guide them to a landing site. They are aligned in the same pattern as the constellation Orion – the home of the ancient space travellers.*

But, Mr Learned Writer, after navigating for light years across the galaxy why would they need a couple of million cubic metres of stone to home in on? (All right, Google Earth hadn't been invented, but they must still have been pretty proficient navigators.)

The capstones on the top of the pyramids are called pyramidions. The Learned Writers are simply pyramidiots.

BRIEF TIMELINE

THE DAWNING OF THE PHARAOHS

3150 BC Dynasty Zero and Narmer is pharaoh of upper and lower Egypt.

2686 BC Building starts on the 'Step' Pyramid.

2589 BC Now the Great Pyramid is started by King Khufu.

2558 BC And then it's the turn of the Sphinx to be constructed.

---

* Are they aligned like Orion? Only if you are in spacecraft, ten miles above the Earth, lying on your back while looking at Egypt over your shoulder through a mirror. It's rocket science.

2498 BC	Papyrus invented as well as mummification.
2400 BC	Meanwhile in Europe they get around to building Stonehenge.
2200 BC	Climate turns hotter and there is desertification. Food supplies fall. In Egypt the Old Kingdom is dying.

The King of South Nile had a tall white crown and he was probably the one who conquered the red-crowned King of North Nile. And at last we have a name for the king of a north–south united country: Narmer. The first of the 'pharaohs' … maybe.

He's the first to be depicted with the red and white crowns together. His symbols are a catfish and a chisel – a 'nar' and a 'mer' in hieroglyphics – giving him the name we know him by: Narmer. His mates probably just called him 'Catfish'. Or 'Chisel'.

— NARMER (3000 BC) —
Pre-Dynasty

Narmer may have conquered the northern half of Egypt, or simply married into it.

> 'A successful man is one who makes more money than his wife can spend. A successful woman is one who can find such a man.'
>
> *Lana Turner (1921–95), American film actress*

Narmer married Neithhotep and her name appears on inscriptions. That (say the Egyptologists) makes her the first woman in history to be named. (Biblical scholars might argue the honour belongs to 'Eve', but let them argue that one.)

He was clearly a man you wouldn't want to cross. In one portrayal he's shown alongside decapitated prisoners of war. In another he is pictured leading a captive by a rope through the victim's nose. Ouch. He is depicted as tearing down walls of enemy fortresses and smacking prisoners over the head with his mace.

Every picture tells a story – especially if you are an illiterate peasant – and Narmer's pictogram message has been repeated down the ages in every language: 'Your mighty monarch will protect you from the enemy – in return you will obey him.'*

Of course it was no picnic being a pharaoh. They faced their own dangerous days. Narmer's successor, Hor-Aha, reigned 62 years before he was eaten by a hippo. But before you shed too many tears for the crinkly king, you have to remember he was probably out *hunting* a hippo that turned the tables. A classic example of the biter bit.

On the Nile, crocodile

If a hippo hadn't feasted on the pharaoh then a crocodile might. Crocodiles divided Egyptian opinions. In some parts of the country the repugnant reptilians were regarded with religious respect.

---

* That is to say, pay him a share of your wealth (let's call it tax) so he can live in luxury. You may also be called upon to fight and die for him.

'Those who live near Thebes keep one crocodile in particular, who is taught to be tame and tractable. They adorn his ears with ear-rings of molten stone or gold, and put bracelets on his forepaws.* They give him a daily portion of bread with a certain number of victims. Having treated him with the greatest possible attention while alive, they embalm him when he dies and bury him in a scared tomb. The people of the Elephantine, on the other hand, are so far from considering the animals sacred that they even eat their flesh.'

Herodotus (484–425 BC), Greek historian

In other regions crocodile-hunting was a pharaoh's way to pass the time. It was brutal for the crocs and dangerous for the hunters. Animal lovers, look away now …

'The hunters bait a hook with a loin of pork and let the meat be carried into the middle of the stream. The hunter on the bank holds a living pig which he beats with a stick. The crocodile hears the pig's cries and heads for the sound. It encounters the pork bait which it instantly swallows down. The men on shore haul it in and plaster its eyes with mud. Once accomplished the creature can be dispatched with ease, otherwise he gives great trouble.'

Herodotus

---

* There's a job you don't often see advertised in your local Job Centre: 'Beautician required to pierce the ears of sacred crocodiles. Candidates must possess a thick skin. Handbag-makers need not apply.'

They must have regarded it as pest control because crocodile meat wasn't a staple food – apparently it needs delicate cooking if you like your steaks tender.

Of course croc meat COULD have been a feast for a fun-loving pharaoh. As the people of the Elephantine region never said …

> 'Give me a crocodile sandwich, and make it snappy.'
>
> *Groucho Marx (1890–1977), US comedian*

— DJER (3000 BC) —
1st Dynasty*

> 'Power always thinks that it is doing God's service when it is violating all his laws.'
>
> *John Adams (1735–1826), 2nd US president*

The hippo's dinner, Hor-Aha, was followed by another long-living pharaoh: Djer. The Egyptians had already evolved the belief that after death their pharaoh moved on from this life to an afterlife. Most religions believe that. But the nasty twist to the Ancient Egyptian faith was that the king still required all the luxuries of this life in the next life.

These included servants. How does a servant serve in the next life? By leaving this life. Djer's tomb is surrounded

---

* Egypt historians organise Egyptian family lines into 'dynasties' just as medieval historians called European ruling families Bourbons or Plantagenets or Tudors. Egyptian families have numbers instead of names. The lists of pharaohs are inaccurate but they serve to give us a sequence, an order. People with OCD find that especially welcome.

by over 300 satellite tombs of retainers who were killed to attend to his needs in Egyptian heaven. This wasteful practice would eventually be replaced by having mummiform figures – *ushabtis* – placed in the graves. That was no consolation to the 300 victims of Djer. Imagine walking in their shoes (or sandals), knowing that when he dies, you die. You'd be executed for doing nothing but your job.

When Djer's tomb was excavated in 1901 – long after it had been robbed – a mummified arm was found in a hidden crack. (Maybe an early robber had stuffed it there, hoping to retrieve it later.) It was the arm of a small woman with four fine gold and amethyst-encrusted bracelets on the wrist. One of the king's wives had gone to her grave with Djer.

> 'I was a queen, and you took away my crown; a wife, and you killed my husband; a mother, and you deprived me of my children. My blood alone remains: take it, but do not make me suffer long.'
>
> *Marie Antoinette (1755–93), Queen of France* *****

* Famous for callously saying, 'Let them eat cake' (when told that the peasants had no bread). In fact there is no record of her saying that. The philosopher Rousseau (1712–78) DID write: 'a great princess was told that the peasants had no bread, and responded: "Let them eat brioche."' But Rousseau wrote that when Marie Antoinette was just a child and clearly didn't mean her. Throw mud and it sticks – the guillotined queen is stuck with that quote.

DYNASTIES 3 TO 6
THE OLD KINGDOM
(2686–2181 BC)

— KHASEKHEMWY (2690 BC) —
2nd Dynasty, and
— DJOSER (2668–2649 BC) —
3rd Dynasty

'Canst thou, O partial sleep, give thy repose
To the wet sea-boy in an hour so rude,
And … Deny it to a king? …
Uneasy lies the head that wears a crown.'

William Shakespeare (1564–1616), English playwright, poet:
Henry IV Part 2

It's all very well being a pampered prince with all the wealth in the world at your disposal. But, as Henry IV says, how do you sleep at night knowing so many people are after your crown?

Pharaoh Khasekhemwy faced enemies inside Egypt as well as outside. Once he'd routed the rebels inside, and invaders from the north, he seems to have decided the best policy was attack. Under Khasekhemwy, Egypt would be looking to conquer new lands. He also dealt with rebellion in Nubia at the southern end of the Nile. That gold-rich region would be a problem for Egypt again … and again and again.

Egypt under Khasekhemwy became richer. The pharaoh faced a new problem. Like a lottery winner today, he had to struggle with the agonising problem: 'How do I spend all that wealth?'

His answer was to build the most impressive funerary complex seen to date.* The dressed stone that lined the tomb made it the largest stone edifice in the world at the time. He was the earliest Egyptian king known to have built statues of himself. It was an idea that would catch on.

Khasekhemwy hadn't invented the iconic pyramid, of course, but he was the herald of the pyramid age. It would be taken on to the next stage by Djoser, the man who was probably his son and who ruled *c.* 2670 BC.

Djoser's monument

Djoser's pyramid was the first all-stone building in the world. Impressive. As a sanctuary for his mummified body it was less of a success. All that remains of him is a mummified left foot.

The robbers of his tomb may not have revered him for his pyramid-building exploits, but his ancestors did. Over a thousand years after Djoser died, a pharaoh compiled a parchment list of kings. A scroll of black ink. But when it came to Djoser's name the scribe switched pens and wrote his name in red ink; the founder of a new era, the age of the pyramids.

---

* Yes, I know that when you win the lottery a gigantic tomb is probably not top of your bucket list. You want your Ferrari, mansion and world cruise in this life. But you're not Khasekhemwy. He was a god and wasn't planning to die.

Did you know ... pretty maids all in a row

King Sneferu (2613–2589 BC) was bored. It's tough at the top. His magician, Djadjamankh, suggested he order 20 beautiful girls to row him across the palace lake. They were draped in nothing but fishing nets. (This is certainly one way of being entertained when there's nothing on daytime television.)

Unfortunately one careless maiden lost her hair clip in the lake as they rowed across. Djadjamankh was ordered to find it. Not a problem for a magician. He folded the lake in half and walked across to the collect the clip. (And there are fairies at the bottom of my garden.)

PYRAMID MAKERS

― ONWARDS AND UPWARDS ―

> 'As a camel beareth labour, and heat, and hunger,
> and thirst, through deserts of sand, and fainteth not;
> so the fortitude of a man shall sustain him through
> all perils.'
>
> *Akhenaton (1351–1334 BC), Egyptian pharaoh*

The earliest pharaohs had tombs rather like the palaces they inhabited when they were alive – single-storey affairs that looked like the mud benches Egyptians constructed at the front of their houses – mastabas. So those early graves were known as mastabas too.

Then along came the 3rd Dynasty of pharaohs and their tombs became upwardly mobile. All those mastabas seemed little more than ripples on the immeasurable, dusty plains. King Djoser had his burial monument constructed higher than the surrounding land, on a ridge – a tomb with a view?

Naturally it needed a creative genius to make it work – the pharaohs clearly didn't have any spare brain cells to design and project-manage massive stone buildings. (After all, they were the men who were stupid enough to believe sacrificing servants for post-mortem duties was a good idea.)

Pharaoh Djoser's go-to man was his vizier (or chief minister) Imhotep. This was the man he consulted about everything, it seemed. The pharaoh went to him to ask how to end a seven-year famine. (Echoes of the Joseph dream story.)

> 'There is no higher religion than human service.'
>
> *Woodrow Wilson (1856–1924), 28th US president*

Imhotep stacked mastaba on top of mastaba till there were six layers like a six-step, four-sided staircase. It's now known as the Step Pyramid.

Inside it was a honeycomb of passages and the entrance was plugged with a three-ton block of granite.* Some of the passages and shafts were occupied by members of the royal family. They included a child of eight.

Topping the tomb with ever-decreasing mastabas was meant to leave Djoser's resting place inaccessible to human hands. It didn't work. His pyramid, like every other in Egypt, has been entered and pillaged many times through history.

When the site was excavated in 1934, by Jean-Philippe Lauer, Djoser's left foot and ankle were all that remained. (A trunkless leg and nothing beside remains?)

Beside the plugged main entrance is a shrine with a statue

---

* Many of these tunnels we see today were dug by tomb-robbers, so it's hard to distinguish the originals. That must have been such hard work – and the punishments for being caught were so severe – you have to wonder if it was worth their efforts. Wouldn't it be easier to get a job?

of Djoser inside. The door has two small holes, not for the curious to peer in but for the king's spirit to circulate outside. Priests would place offerings in front of the shrine, Djoser would enjoy the 'spirit' of the food, and then the priests would tuck in to the actual food for supper.

> 'For famous men have the whole earth as their memorial.'
>
> *Pericles (495–429 BC), Greek statesman and general*

Grand designer Imhotep went on to be revered as a god himself. But his remains have never been found. Not even a foot. Not even a talented toe. However, he was remembered well into the Roman period as a sage, magician, healer and scribe. He was remembered long after his fellow Old Kingdom Egyptians were forgotten – a fitting memorial for the man who created the prototype of the country's defining symbol: the pyramid.

— SNEFERU —
(2613–2589 BC) and
— KHUFU —
(2589–2566 BC), 4th Dynasty

> 'I think God, in creating man, somewhat overestimated his ability.'
>
> *Oscar Wilde (1854-1900), Irish writer and poet*

Keeping up with the Joneses is not a new social quest. Pharaoh Sneferu built three huge pyramids – the Red pyramid, the Meidum pyramid and the Bent pyramid – you can see from the last that they hadn't quite got the hang of straight-sided pyramids yet. The bottom half is regular but the upper half bends inwards as if the builders were in a hurry to get to the pointy bit at the top.

The German archaeologist Ludwig Borchardt (1863–1938) said the king must have died suddenly and the builders had to rush to finish it. But Ludwig, like a lot of his Victorian colleagues, was really only guessing. The mass of stones needed to build it 'bent' is not much less than that needed to build it straight.

And, anyway, Sneferu's northern (or 'Red' pyramid) was built AFTER the Bent pyramid. Sneferu wouldn't be commissioning that when he was dead … unless, of course, he really WAS a god.

> 'Each one prays to God according to his own light.'
>
> *Mahatma Gandhi (1869–1948), Indian nationalist*

Those pyramids of Sneferu were the most impressive buildings the ancient world had ever seen. His son and heir, Khufu, just had to build a bigger one – the 'Great Pyramid of Giza', in fact. So 'great' it became the tallest man-made structure in the world for over 3,800 years.*

The statistics are impressive but meaningless without a context.† So thank you, Napoleon Bonaparte, for giving the world a powerful image. Boney was in Egypt in 1798, doing his usual conquering act, when he got to view the pyramids

---

* If you're ever asked in a pub quiz, 'What was the first building that eventually topped the Great Pyramid?' then it was Lincoln Cathedral around AD 1300.

† The odd statistic DOES catch me by surprise. The fact that the Great Pyramid required half a million tons of mortar. Mortar? Yes, the massive stones were cemented in place like a brick wall. You can imagine an Egyptian boy from the blackstuff applying for a job? 'Giza job?'

at Giza. As his officers climbed to the top he sat in the shade and did a sum … long before calculators had been invented. Napoleon reckoned the stone from the three pyramids would build a wall around France that was a foot thick (0.3 metres) and 12 foot high (3.7 metres).*

Another calculation says that if the Great Pyramid were chopped into 12-inch cubes, and those cubes were joined end to end, there would be enough to circle the moon almost three times. (All you'd need would be a cement mixer that worked in a low-gravity environment.)

Did you know … pyramid prediction

Napoleon was led into the heart of the Khufu pyramid by an Egyptian guide. He suddenly dismissed the man, saying (in French), 'I vont to be alone.'

He seemed to spend an inordinate amount of time in the lantern-lit heart of the tomb. When he finally emerged he was pale and shaking. The guide asked if he was all right and Napoleon snapped, 'Don't ever mention this again.'

It was much later in his eventful life that Napoleon himself raised the matter. He hinted that he'd had a vision in there and it may have revealed his own future. Tantalisingly he refused to say more until … he lay dying. 'Inside the Pyramid of Khufu … but no … what's the use? You'd never believe me … gurgle, gurgle, death-rattle.'

---

* Careful with those measurements. We say that an overcompensating short person has a 'Napoleon complex'. The history books consistently cite Napoleon's height as 5 feet, 2 inches (1.6 metres). But that's because they mistakenly believed that a French 'foot' was the same as an English foot. Correctly converted, Napoleon soars to a towering 5 feet, 7 inches (1.7 metres). You wouldn't pick him for your basketball team, but nor would you cast him in your *War and Peace* movie to play … erm … Napoleon.

The point of the pyramid

'Give me problems, give me the most abstruse
cryptogram or the most intricate analysis, and I am
in my own proper atmosphere. I abhor the dull
routine of existence.'

Sherlock Holmes, character in The Sign of Four *by Arthur Conan
Doyle (1859–1930), Scottish doctor and writer*

Khufu's pyramid is a mystery Sherlock Holmes never
attempted to crack. Not so much 'Who-murdered-the-body-
in-the-library' as 'Where-is-the-bleedin'-body, Watson?'

In AD 820 the Caliph of Baghdad arrived in Egypt to
follow a legend of hidden treasure the way the Conquistadors
would seek out Eldorado in South America 600 years
later. The stories the Caliph heard said there were fabulous
treasures hidden in 30 chambers in the Great Pyramid.*

His excavators found a 350-foot-long passageway that
ended in a large chamber. In the corner was a pit and another
passage that led 50 foot … to what? A dead end.

He traced another passage to two more chambers and in
the final one there lay a stone coffin – the sarcophagus. No
treasure. And no mummified body. Only an empty coffin.

The Victorians revisited the pyramid to solve the mystery
of why it was built. What they couldn't prove, they invented.
The pyramidologists claimed the Pyramid of Khufu was …

◪ An observatory for star-gazing and calculating
calendars.

---

* There were golden treasures but also practical ones like maps of Earth
and the stars as well as fabled treasures such as unbreakable glass.

◪ A sundial – maybe Khufu couldn't find one in his local garden centre.

◪ A horoscope calculator – an Institute of Pyramidology claims they can show how it predicted major earthly events such as the crucifixion of Christ and the First World War.*

◪ A series of waiting rooms for Christian souls on their way to heaven or hell … even though it was built a couple of thousand years before Christ was born.

◪ A symbol of the oppressive might of the priests – a bit like a Norman cathedral: 'Look on our works and despair.' The priests (the pyramidologists argued) conned Khufu into paying for it but had no intention of actually burying him there.

These theories are as nutty as a Brazil-nut tree. The truth is, no one really knows why Khufu didn't end up in his massive mausoleum.

The masterful masons

Statistics on the Great Pyramid are mind-boggling. For example, the builders would have had to put a block of stone in place every two to three minutes, working a ten-hour day, seven days a week, for the duration of Khufu's reign.

But the one statistic never calculated is, 'How much did it cost?' The answer is, 'It cost Khufu his reputation.' So much of the nation's time and effort went into the Great Pyramid that the rest of the buildings were neglected. The Egyptians were harsh in their judgement.

---

* But nothing really useful like next week's winning lottery numbers.

'Khufu brought the country into all sorts of misery. He closed the temples, forbade his subjects to offer sacrifices, and compelled them without exception to labour on his works. The Egyptians can barely bring themselves to mention his name, so great is their hatred.'

Herodotus

So while modern visitors gaze on its wonders they have little idea that the Great Pyramid was so detested in its own era.

Did you know... the overseer

The man who acted as Khufu's pyramid project-manager was his nephew Hemiunu. A full-time job, you would think. Yet as well as supervising the building of the pyramid he found time to hold other titles: priest to the gods and goddesses the Cat, the Lion, the Panther, the Ram of Mendes, and Keeper of the Bull of Apis (he could have built a zoo for that lot). He was high priest of Thoth – God of Wisdom. Yet he *still* found time for another job: 'Director of Music to the South and the North.'

His reward for his efforts was to have his own pyramid built near the Great one. His statues show an obese man – obesity being a symbol of fat-cat success. It demonstrated that, while the peasants laboured on a subsistence diet, Hemiunu had a surplus of food and fat (cholesterol and chins).

Hemiunu's obesity may have been a source of pride. It was probably a source of death too.

When it was finished, the Great Pyramid of Khufu was clad in a white limestone that must have dazzled in the desert sun.

What happened to the white cladding? It was pinched to build Cairo.

Pyramid power

> 'Man fears Time, but Time fears the Pyramids.'
>
> *Egyptian proverb*

The pyramids are forever the symbol of Ancient Egypt. Thousands of years later they were being built by the Mayans and Aztecs in Central America. That led to some pyramidologists making a link between the cultures.

The believers argue that simple Mayan farmers could never have built those pyramids. The Egyptians must have sailed across the Atlantic Ocean 2,000 years before Columbus and settled in Mexico.

Sensible historians like you and I may mock. But on 1 September 1996 a sensational story appeared in the newspapers. It said that traces of cocaine and tobacco had been found in Egyptian mummies.

It seemed to indicate the pharaohs smoked tobacco or chewed coca leaves – the source of cocaine – plants only found in the New World.

German scientist Svetlana Balabanova did not believe the results when she tested the mummies from British and German museums.

> 'The results were a shock. I was sure it was a mistake.'
>
> *Svetlana Balabanova, German toxicologist*

But she was convinced after repeating the tests.* Some Egyptologists kept an open mind.

> 'We have always said there is no evidence of links between Egypt and the Americas – but there is never any evidence until it appears.'
>
> Rosalie David, Keeper of Egyptology at Manchester Museum

Others were scathing about the idea that the Egyptians sailed the Atlantic thousands of years before Columbus.

> 'The idea that the Egyptians should have travelled to America is overall absurd, and I also don't know anyone who spends time doing research in these areas, because they're not perceived to be areas that have any real meaning for the subjects.'
>
> John Baines, Egyptologist (1997)

Could the Egyptians really have sailed the oceans? Evidence is emerging that they could. Around 1477 BC, Queen Hatshepsut funded a mysterious overseas expedition to the Land of Punt, which is pictured in a relief at Deir el-Bahari (in modern-day Luxor). It shows five ships, each measuring about 20 metres long, carrying 210 men and loaded with gold, trees and exotic animals which can only be found along the coast of Africa.

Then, in 2011, archaeologists excavating a dried-up lagoon unearthed traces of an ancient harbour that once launched early voyages like Hatshepsut's onto the open ocean. Inside

---

* Balabanova examined the mummy of a female priestess called Henut Taui. If she was on cocaine she must have been a high priestess. Sorry, I'll get my coat.

a series of man-made caves they found timber, rigging, limestone anchors, steering oars, reed mats, cedar planks, and the remains of the oldest seagoing ships ever discovered.

So in theory South American drugs *could* have reached Egypt. Did the Egyptians reciprocate by giving the Mayans the idea of pyramids?

Unlikely, because Egyptian pyramids are carefully engineered, built from solid stone so they cover a tomb inside. Mayan pyramids are piles of sand and rubble, covered with a stone face so they can place an altar on the top.

Other writers have said the Mayan people were Alexander the Great's Greek sailors – who turned right in the Mediterranean instead of left and got a little lost.

In the 1960s a Swiss writer came up with a new theory. The beings who planned the Mayan pyramids weren't human. They were the same aliens from outer space who had built the Egyptian pyramids. The Mayan pyramid platforms would make landing pads for their flying saucers.

This may sound wacky and fantastic to you. But remember … he sold an awful lot of books!

Did you know … pyramid passions

The Greek historian Herodotus is known as 'The Father of History' as well as 'The Father of Lies'. Though he visited Egypt in c. 450 BC, he's not the most reliable source of stories.

He reported that King Cheops made his daughter sit in a bedroom and charge men for her favours. She charged each man a block of stone. She then used these to build a pyramid near the Great Pyramid with sides almost 50 metres long. That's an awful lot of love.

Pyramid pinching

> 'Economy does not lie in sparing money, but in spending it wisely.'
>
> *Thomas Huxley (1825–95), English biologist*

Amenemhet III of the 12th Dynasty (ruled 1842–1797 BC) broke the mould of pharaohs and decided to have his pyramid built from mud bricks. This was then cased with limestone so it looked like the great stone pyramids. It was pyramid building on the cheap. Be warned, it is a false economy if you plan your memorial to last for all time.

Amenemhet III should have known that those bright limestone facing stones were irresistible to thieves.

Once the cladding vanished from Amenemhet III's tomb, the mud bricks were eroded by wind and sandstorms. What's left is not so much a pyramid as a blob on the landscape.

⌐ THE POWER OF THE PYRAMIDS ⌐

> 'I'm building a glass pyramid over the Egyptian escalator where my body will be mummified, so my customers can come and see me forever.'
>
> *Mohamed Al-Fayed (1929—),*
> *Egyptian businessman and former owner of Harrods store* ✱

✱ Presumably the plan to attract customers to his store with his corpse on display has been abandoned since he sold the store in 2010. He reacted angrily when he had trouble getting the board to approve his dividend payment. 'I can't take my profit because I have to take a permission of those bloody idiots,' he explained politely. We may never now see that glass pyramid. Such a loss.

There are mysterious forces at work in this world. They are invisible to normal mortals like thee and me. But to the pyramidiots they are as real as a bacon sandwich.

We know the original pyramid was built in ever-decreasing squares of mud-brick walls. That 'step pyramid' shape was then smoothed off to give the shape we recognise today.

But, against that sensible sequence, the pyramidiots say the pyramid shape was always meant to be. Why? Because the pyramid shape itself is magical. The very shape focuses invisible forces of the universe and generates a force field that is more powerful than anything humans can devise. Or, to put it in simple terms that any pyramidiot can comprehend…

> 'Pyramids act as an effective resonator of randomly polarised microwave signals which can be converted into electrical energy.'
> Patrick Flanagan (1944—), American New Age author and inventor

By rigorous (or not so rigorous) experiment it has been demonstrated that pyramids …

◁▷ **Preserve.** Legend has it that a French shopkeeper called Antoine Bovis visited the Great Pyramid of Giza in the 1930s. (He denied any such visit and says his experiments were conducted in France.) The story goes on that he found the pyramid had been visited by a legion of loutish tourists who had left litter strewn around. It had also been entered by a stray cat that had chosen this spot to die. Bovis noticed something amazing about the corpse of the cat. It had not decomposed as it should have done. It was all but mummified even though it had never been through an embalming process. What explanation could he come up with? The pyramid itself had preserved puss. It was a focus for forces unknown.* He went back to France and experimented. What is certain is that Bovis claimed to have constructed model pyramids and left different types of food inside them. He found that all the food stayed in good condition for much longer than anyone would expect.

> 'With the help of our positive 2000° magnetic plates we can mummify small animals, could the pyramid have the same property? I tried, and as you can observe with the small fish and the little piece of meat still hanging, I succeeded totally.'
>
> *Antoine Bovis*

◁▶ **Sharpen.** In 1949, an engineer from Czechoslovakia, Karel Drbal, studied Bovis's experiments. He wondered if the pyramid would preserve metal the way it preserved food. Razor blades were in short supply in his country in those days. So he put blades under a model pyramid to see if it would stop them getting blunt.† He went so far as to patent the idea of his little pyramids as razor-sharpeners. Drbal was not original though. In fact he was years behind *The Times*:

---

* Or it was cool and dry inside the tunnels – like a larder in an old house. That explanation didn't satisfy the brilliant Bovis. Perhaps we don't have the insight of the Bovis brain. Maybe we need to stick our heads inside a pyramid?

† Drbal's pyramids are made of cardboard. You can make one yourself if you have a spare hour and a sheet of cardboard to waste. You can even try to market them to razor-blade users. But be careful, it's a cut-throat business.

> 'If I oriented my razor blade N. and S. by the compass
> they tend to last considerably longer. The idea of
> keeping razor blades in a magnetic field is not quite
> new. I found this out about the year 1900.'
>
> *Letter to* The Times, *1933*

◁▶ **Symbolise**. Secret, mystical societies have used the pyramid as a symbol of their quasi religions. They make mystical pronouncements like …

> 'The Pyramid originally symbolises illumination*
> and the road to illumination becomes narrower and
> narrower the higher up you reach. Eventually you
> pass through the illumination of the sun to ultimate
> illumination on the other side.'

◁▶ **Improve**. A wine-producer in western Canada built a four-storey replica of the Great Pyramid in order to improve the quality of wine aged inside. You could really impress your friends by claiming to taste the difference. Of all the pretentions of wine tasting, the most appropriate comment for a pyramid wine is …

> 'Solid structure!'

That is a catch-all phrase to sum up wine where four components are equal: acid balanced against sweetness; fruit balanced against tannin.†

---

* No it doesn't (you could argue). It is a pointy structure symbolising nothing.

† NOT that wine tasters ever slide into pretentiousness. Oh, no. Some of their judgements are illuminating. You can hold your friends in awe by

◁▶ **Stimulate**. Sit or sleep under a pyramid and your brainpower will increase. A form of meditation called 'Transmission Meditation' requires you to sit under a metal-poled tetrahedron. You can then tune into cosmic energy radiating from a cosmic entity.* The gullible will also be filling the wallets of the manufacturers of the pole pyramid. Yet American pyramid-lovers have been known to attend lectures with paper pyramids on their heads. They are sure it enhances their mental power.

Peril of the pyramids

Every state project in Ancient Egypt – a pyramid or a temple – had a crew of workers. Each was responsible for one part of the pyramid complex. Each crew of workers was divided into four or five smaller units, which Egyptologists call 'phyles' (after the Greek word for 'tribe'). Each phyle carried a name, such as 'Great One' or 'Green One'. The phyles in turn were broken into forces of 10 to 20 men, and these had names like 'Endurance' and 'Perfection'. They clearly took pride in their work and enjoyed the camaraderie of being part of a team.

Archaeologists have discovered that pyramid-building was a dangerous day's work. They had accidents while building the pyramids. Zahi Hawass, Director General of Giza, said, 'We found 12 skeletons

---

simply learning and reciting the following: 'There's the faintest soupçon of asparagus and just a flutter of Edam cheese.' (Quote from the movie *Sideways*, 2004.)

* Does that not sound wonderful? But beware. The proponents of this say some people are so energised that they cannot cope with the dynamo effects they experienced. If you are one of those, it may be better if you twiddle radio dials and tune into a cosmic entity called Radio 2.

who had accidents with their hands, doctors made splints of wood. One worker suffered a badly injured arm, which a doctor amputated below the elbow. Another skeleton showed a stone had fallen down on his leg, and they did a kind of operation. It involved cutting open the leg. It must have worked because both men lived more than ten years after their operation.'

There are no records or tomb paintings showing women pushing stones and statues on sleds (as there are of men doing this kind of work). Yet the condition of some women's skeletons suggest they were. There is more damage to their bones than you would expect from doing household chores.

The typical lifespan of the pyramid worker was 30 to 35 years.

— KHAFRE —

(ruled c. 2570 BC), 4th Dynasty

AND THE SPHINX SQUEEZE

> 'I embrace my rival, but only to strangle him.'
>
> *Jean Racine (1639–99), French dramatist*

Khufu's son, Khafre, built a second pyramid on the same Giza plain as his father's Great Pyramid. It was built on higher ground so it looks bigger. In fact it is 10 metres shorter.

Khafre also built the colossal statue of a creature with the body of a lion and a human head. The mythical Sphinx.*

---

* The Greek version of this monster had wings and a reputation for being

This benevolent beast guarded the entrance to Khafre's temple. Most experts agree its defaced face is that of Khafre himself.

We don't know what the Egyptians called this statue. 'Sphinx' was a Greek label applied 2,000 years after it was erected. The word probably stems from the Greek, meaning 'to squeeze'. The Greek Sphinx had an unfortunate penchant for strangling humans.

As with most fabled monuments the Khafre Sphinx has a legend of its own. That widely believed legend says that the sphinx sat in the desert for thousands of years until along came Napoleon's army. The French soldiers took one look at the stony visage, formed an instant dislike for it and used it as target practice for their cannon. They blew its nose off ... and it's not nice to have your nose picked on.

The truth is the idea of blaming Napoleon is easily blown apart. The damage happened 500 years before the French arrived.

In 1378 the Arab tribes were led by Mohammed Sa'im al-Dahr – a Muslim who was enraged to find the Egyptian peasants praying to the statue. Reputedly he attacked the sphinx single-handed with a chisel. (He didn't need scaffolding or ladders because years of sandstorms had left the statue buried up to its neck.) The manic message from Sa'im al-Dahr was clear: 'So much for your false idol.'

What happened next? The crops in that region failed for many years and desert sands covered the area. Sa'im al-Dahr was hanged for his vandalism. No wonder the sphinx has an enigmatic smile.

---

treacherous as a turncoat and merciless as a traffic warden. It was female, unlike the Egyptian model, and feasted on the flesh of those who failed to answer its enigmatic question. Again like the traffic warden ... 'Is this your car, sir?'

In the 1700s Mamaluk soldiers from Egypt turned their guns on the statue and that may have led to the tale of Napoleon and a shot sphinx, which persists in school books to this day.

Did you know ... gunpowder plot

Richard Vyse (1784–1853) was an early Egyptologist. When he came to a sealed tomb he used gunpowder to blast his way through. In the Great Pyramid of Giza he spent over three months detonating his way into new chambers. Despite his crude methods he made some important discoveries, such as a chamber containing graffiti written by the work gangs; he also uncovered the name of the Great Pyramid's pharaoh, Khufu.

Vyse – a vandal or a pioneer? Today the chamber also contains a fair amount of 19th- and 20th-century graffiti. Definitely vandals.

— UNAS —
(2375–2345 BC), 5th Dynasty

> 'There is no humiliation more abusive than hunger.'
>
> *Pranab Mukherjee (1935—), President of India*

The life of Pharaoh Unas is not very well recorded, but his death was accompanied by 'The Pyramid Texts'. They give us an insight into the religion of the old kingdom as well as the daily life.

The inscriptions include one known as 'The Cannibal Hymn'. A cheerful ditty that translates as …

> 'Unas is the one who eats men and gods.
> Unas eats their magic and swallows their spirits.
> Their big ones are for his breakfast,
> Their middle ones are for his dinner,
> The little ones for his supper,
> And the old men and women are fuel for his fire.'

So the old folk don't end up in a Unas care-home, they become the toast of the town. But if Unas was well fed then the most famous images from his tomb show the opposite.

The depictions of poor people in a time of famine are just as grim as the pharaoh cannibal's eating habits:

- An emaciated man is supported by his skinny wife as he lies dying.

- A boy with a swollen belly begs a woman for food.

- Another woman is driven to eating the lice in her hair to survive.

Unas can't have been depicting the Egyptian people under his rule. The suffering starvelings must have been people of the desert – the images are a reminder to the people of Egypt just how lucky they are to be under the protection of their pharaoh. 'There, but for the grace of Unas the god, go you.'

⁓ PEPI II ⁓
(2278–2184 BC), 6th Dynasty

> 'Old age is no place for sissies.'
>
> *Bette Davis (1908–89), American actress*

No one can agree on how long Pensioner Pepi ruled. Most agree he came to the throne at the age of six, but did he rule for a further 64 or 94 years? (Some argue the figure '94' was a clerical error as it looks so much like '64' in hieroglyphic scripts.)

What we do know is that as a boy-king he had a perverse fascination with dwarfs. He sent an expedition south into deepest Africa to trade in ivory and ebony. When Pepi II heard his expedition leader had captured a pygmy, he was ecstatic.

The pharaoh wrote to the captain of the pygmy prison ship to tell him how to treat the man as they sailed down the Nile's miles. You can hear the excitement in the Pepi pen as he writes …

'You have said that you have brought a pygmy from the land of the horizon-dwellers. You have said to my majesty that his like has never been brought by anyone who went to Yam previously. Come north to my palace at once! Hurry and bring with you this pygmy whom you brought from the land of the horizon-dwellers live, hail and healthy, for the dances of the god, to gladden the heart, to delight the heart of King Pepi Neferkare who lives forever!

'When he goes down with you into the ship, get

worthy men to be around him on deck, lest he fall
into the water. When he lies down at night, get
worthy men to lie around him in his tent. Inspect
him ten times at night. My majesty desires to see this
pygmy more than the gifts of the mine-land and of
Punt. When you arrive at the palace and this pygmy
is with you alive, fit and healthy, my majesty will do
great things for you, more than was done for the
god's seal-bearer.'

Tomb inscription

The thoughts of the imprisoned pygmy are not recorded.
Was he happy or grumpy? If he was to dance for the pharaoh,
let's hope he wasn't bashful, eh?*

The pygmy was the highlight (or low-light, if you are being
dwarfist) of the expedition. The exploration 1,000 miles
south of Egypt had been led by Harkhuf, Chief of Scouts.†
Harkhuf led expeditions through hostile Nubians to Yam
and traded with the chief of Yam. He returned with panther
skins and elephant tusks – no worries about endangered
species in those days. He brought back incense and ebony,
precious oils and throw-sticks.

He was so successful he returned a second time ... though
he may have had a secret motive: to spy on the rebellious
Nubian statelets. He was disappointed to find the chief of
Yam was not at home but away fighting a neighbouring tribe.

---

* Those are the names given by the Walt Disney film writers to Snow
White's dwarfs, of course. The original Grimm tale didn't name them.
Then, in a 1912 *Snow White* stage play, they were named as Blick, Flick,
Glick, Snick, Plick, Whick and Quee. The play was performed on West
44th Street, New York City ... at 'The Little Theatre'. It just had to be.
† Not to be confused with Robert Baden-Powell, Chief Scout, who
taught boys woodcraft skills. In BP's youth organisation boys learned how
to make fire by rubbing two cubs together.

Harkhuf was not deterred. He set off to the battlefield, met the chief of Yam and traded with him there.

As he returned to Egypt the Nubians were waiting like a troupe of Dick Turpins to rob him. Luckily the Yam chief had given Harkhuf an escort. He survived. Being an explorer to the pharaohs made you endure as many dangerous days as being a warrior.

It was on the third trip for Pepi that the famous pygmy prize was landed. Harkhuf was so proud of that excited letter from Pepi II he had the full text inscribed on the wall of his tomb.*

Did you know ... dong gone

The 19th Dynasty Pharaoh Menephta (1213–1203 BC) defeated the Libyan army in the sixth year of his reign and wanted trophies and counters of the dead enemy soldiers. He ordered their penises to be harvested. He had his way ... because where there's a will there's a way. Records list ...

- Phalluses of Libyan generals 6
- Phalluses cut off Libyans 6,359
- Sirculians killed, phalluses cut off 222
- Etruscans killed, phalluses cut off 542
- Greeks killed, phalluses presented to the King 6,111[†]

---

* An interesting idea. What letter would YOU have inscribed on your tombstone? The one confirming your three GCSE results? Your knighthood? Your decree nisi? Or that email from a Nigerian diplomat offering to share his £10 million fortune?

† That's a total of 13,240, in case you were wondering. Napoleon's mathematicians didn't calculate the dimensions of a penis pyramid they could have made. Maybe they thought size doesn't matter.

Faded pharaoh

> 'Reputation is an idle and most false imposition; oft
> got without merit, and lost without deserving.'
>
> *William Shakespeare:* Othello

Sometimes people just live too long. Elizabeth I grew old and stale as the Tudor world declined. Pepi II ruled successfully for years but as his energy faded so Egypt declined. Lesser men made little demesnes within Pepi's empire and rival states outside hovered like vultures.

When Pepi's chancellor went south to confront the Nubian rebels, he was killed. The chancellor's son, Sabni, had to mount a huge expedition to retrieve his father's body – without a properly buried body, he believed, his father's afterlife would be hell.

As Egypt crumbled, so did Pepi's reputation. A story emerged that became one of the most popular in Ancient Egypt. It told of Pepi II's relationship with his general, Sasenet ...

> 'King Pepi was seen going out at night. He threw a
> brick and kicked at a wall as a signal. A rope ladder
> descended and King Pepi climbed it.* Now, after his
> majesty had done what he desired with General
> Sasenet, he returned to his palace.'

A demeaning reputation for the king, who ruled at the end of the pyramid age.

---

* We have to assume this escapade was not carried out when Pepi was in his nineties. The image of a passionate pensioner scaling a wall is an entertaining one though.

DYNASTIES 7 TO 10
THE FIRST INTERMEDIATE PERIOD
(2181–2040 BC)

The 'Intermediate' periods in Ancient Egypt were when the smooth successions were lost in a muddle and confused clutter of kings. Rivals wrestled in un-civil war or invaders intruded to rob, raid or ravage or struggle to settle. For 'Intermediate' period read 'the most dangerous days of all'.

— ANARCHY IN EGYPT —

'Perhaps the less we have, the more we are required to brag.'

John Steinbeck (1902–68), American author: East of Eden

Pepi ruled too long. All his heirs had died before he vacated the royal throne so, when he did finally stroll past the Great Devourer, lesser princes fought for his throne and the civil war almost tore Egypt apart.

Princes in the south fought pharaohs in the Nile Delta for control. But in the far south there was a noble called Ankhtify (during the 9th Dynasty) who decided to take advantage of the chaos to found his own little fiefdom at Hierakonpolis.

If you ever fancy ruling your country then take a tip from Ankhtify – blow your own flugelhorn. Tell people how great you are and eventually they will believe you. Or perhaps Ankhtify just had a massive inferiority complex and the only one he was trying to convince was himself…

'I am the beginning and end of mankind, for my
equal has not and will not come into being. I am the
vanguard of men and the rear-guard of men, a leader
of men through example, strong in speech, practical
in thought. I am an honest man who has no equal, a
man who can talk freely when others are obliged to
be silent.'

Ankhtify, tomb inscription

The Thebans were wary of Ankhtify's military skills and
aggression. Thebes decided not to meet Ankhtify in open
battle. Naturally he took this as a sign of his own strength ...
not their tactical nous.

'Then my courageous troops, yes my bold troops,
ventured to the Theban kingdom, looking for an
open battle. But no one dared to come out from
Thebes because they were afraid of my troops.'

Thebes relied on the old, unbeatable enemy, Death.
Once Ankhtify died, the breakaway black sheep of the
Hierakonpolis flock were returned to the fold.

Life under Ankhtify was as dangerous as anywhere else
in the chaos of the First Intermediate Period. It wasn't just
the brawls and battles. It was the old enemy, hunger, stalking
the land. Again the warlord Ankhtify used it as an excuse
to boast ...

'I gave bread to the hungry and clothing to the naked;
I gave sandals to the barefooted; I gave a wife to him
who had no wife. I took care of the towns when the
sky was clouded and the earth was parched and

when everybody died of hunger. The south came with its people and the north with its children; they brought finest oil in exchange for the barley which was given to them.

'The whole of Upper Egypt died of hunger and each individual had reached such a state of hunger that he ate his own children. But I refused to see anyone die of hunger in my state and gave to the north grain of Upper Egypt. And I do not think that anything like this has been done by the governors who came before me. I brought life to the province of Hierakonpolis.'

With the country in pieces the last thing it needed was a famine. It seems sudden global climate change led to the complete drying up of Lake Faiyum – a major body of water fed by the Nile which was 65 metres deep. It evaporated over a long period from 2200 to 2150 BC, around the start of the Old Kingdom's collapse.

The four horsemen of the Apocalypse always seem to ride out together – Conquest, War, Famine and Death.

It never rains but it pours … except, of course, it didn't pour. And the Old Kingdom died.

MUMMIFIED MONARCHS

— THE MAGIC OF THE MUMMIES —

> 'Knowledge is not necessarily wisdom.'
>
> *Egyptian proverb*

Around 4,000 years ago there was an ancient half-forgotten civilisation that was driven from its homeland in the Sahara when it became desert.*

They seem to have emigrated to the fertile Nile Valley and brought elements of their practices with them. They had animal-headed gods, for example. The most intriguing feature of this shadowy culture is the idea that they had perfected mummification a thousand years before the Egyptians. The Egyptians didn't 'invent' the mummification of the dead – they *copied* it.

---

* The Sahara now extends to 3,630,000 square miles. Roughly the same as the United States of America. (Yet another priceless fact for the pub-quiz enthusiast.)

The evidence is slight but difficult to avoid. A three-year-old boy has been uncovered by archaeologists. He has been embalmed in such a sophisticated way that archaeologists believe this unknown tribe had been refining the process for hundreds of years before they moved to Egypt. The boy is called the Black Mummy ... which is a delightful name for a mummy mystery or a horror film.

Did you know ... damned mummies

Ancient Egyptians were fussy about who would be privileged enough to journey into the afterlife and who wouldn't. Only a preserved, mummified body could make the one-way trip to paradise. Some mummies were physically damaged by their enemies so they'd be refused entry.

Their mouths were deliberately battered so they couldn't speak their name at the afterlife gates and would even struggle to 'breathe'. They were damned for eternity.

— EMBALMING EXPERTISE —

'They first take an iron hook and with it draw out the brain through the nostrils.'*

Herodotus

---

* Embalmers sometimes made an incision just behind the eye and used a scoop to remove the grey matter. A 2014 electronic scan showed one mummy had bits of brain left behind. The embalmer had clearly given the mummy a piece of his mind. A 2014 X-ray revealed another embalmer left the hook of his brain-puller inside the skull. He must have been trained by an NHS surgeon.

Every school pupil knows how to make a mummy.* So let's not dwell on the basics, which you already know, but give special tips for those who wish to practise on a local tax-inspector …

🪲 Take the corpse to 'The Beautiful House' – a large outdoor gazebo in the countryside so the smells can blow away.

🪲 Remove the brain through the nostrils and throw it away – the seat of the mind is the heart and that stays in the body.

🪲 Use a stone knife to open the belly, plunge your arms up to the elbows to extract the internal organs. An embalmer called a 'ripper-up' usually does this.

> 'They take out the whole contents of the stomach which they then clean, washing it with palm wine. After that they fill the hole with myrrh and other spices. They sew up the opening.'
>
> *Herodotus*

🪲 The body is placed in salt for 70 days.† The liver, stomach, intestines and lungs are stored in their own jars, each created in the shape of the appropriate god…

---

* In the more progressive schools they do dramatic re-enactments in which the largest student wraps the smallest student in toilet roll to replicate the embalming process. Sometimes a teacher is actually present and encouraging this.

† Early embalmers used sand, but this left the skin very tight. Later embalmers discovered that natron, a salty chemical found around the sides of lakes near Cairo, did a better job.

🪲 **Duamutef**, the jackal-headed god – the stomach.

🪲 **Qebehsenuef**, the falcon-headed god – the intestines.

🪲 **Hapi**, the baboon-headed god – the lungs.

🪲 **Imseti**, the human-headed god – the liver.

🪲 Prepare the body with make-up and a wig so they look their best in the afterlife. Curling tongs will give the wig a fashionable permed appearance.*

🪲 Wash the body and wrap it round from head to foot with bandages of fine linen cloth smeared with bitumen.†

🪲 Perform the ceremony of the opening-of-the-mouth so the dead one can eat, drink and speak in the afterlife.

Research and technology moves on. X-rays and CT scans allow archaeologists to examine a mummy without unwrapping it and destroying it. We can learn more about their LIVES – the unwrappers only learned more about their death practices.

So what are the top ten things you may NOT know …?

---

* Egyptians used a fatty substance the way modern people use hair gel but they used it in life as well as on mummified corpses. If the love of your life smelled like a bag of chips you might actually lust after him/her with a heightened passion. It's all a matter of taste – and smell.

† 'Mummy' was the Egyptian word for bitumen, hence the name. Those bandages could total 375 square metres – enough to cover a basketball court, though it would make a mess of the ball.

TEN FOUL FACTS ABOUT MUMMIES

'Wisdom is not a product of schooling but of the lifelong attempt to acquire it.'

Albert Einstein (1879–1955), German-born physicist

1   In ancient times only the very rich or powerful earned an easy trip to the afterlife through the embalming process. Later it became a huge industry with even the poorest hoping for it. The downside was you-gets-what-you-pays-for. Your corpse would get a mere week in the drying salt. In fact merely wrapping a body and burying it in the hot Egyptian sands did an excellent preservation job.

2   The cheapest method of cleaning the intestines – the one used by the poorer relatives – was to flush out the bowels with a pipe through the rectum. (An enema of the people, you might say.)

3   It took the Ancient Egyptians about 1,500 years to get the embalming process right. The first mummies were just wrapped in bandages and left to rot. But Egyptian cooks taught the mummy-makers the best way to keep meat fresh was to gut an animal and keep its body in salt. Yummy mummy.

4   Detailed examinations have revealed that the divine pharaohs were not going to win any beauty contests.

Ramesses III had been a very fat man. In fact he was obese and suffered arthritis and dental problems. His cholesterol-clogged arteries probably killed him – that appears to have been a major killer among the rich. He was 90 years old so he can't have had too many complaints. His mummy began to deteriorate once it was unwrapped. It was sent to Paris for restorative work and travelled on an Egyptian passport. Ramesses had his occupation listed as 'King (deceased)'.

DANGEROUS DAYS DEATH I

CHOLESTEROL-CLOGGED ARTERIES

High-class rich living has always been bad for your heart, even in Egyptian times. A diet high in fat causes raised fat levels in your blood, the old 'cholesterol' time bomb.

Over years the 'oil slick' of fats gets deposited on the walls of arteries, gradually clogging them up. When this happens to the major arteries supplying critical body organs like the heart, it's only a matter of time before the blood supply is restricted. Less blood to the heart muscle causes angina pain due to a lack of oxygen, the muscle fuel. Complete blockage kills the heart muscle, causing initially severe crushing chest pain, sweating and vomiting. As the heart dies, fighting for oxygen, you become severely short of breath and your heart stops – cardiac arrest.

Dr Peter Fox MB, ChB, FRCGP, DrCOG

5   Poor dental hygiene was dangerously careless and
a killer. One scan revealed a mummy had so many
abscesses around his teeth his jaw was hollowed out.
The poisoned pus* probably killed him, as it had a lot
of his contemporaries.

> 'My mouth is full of decayed teeth and my soul of
> decayed ambitions.'
>
> *James Joyce (1882–1941), Irish novelist and poet*

6   An eviscerated corpse will shrivel and scare the hell out
of everyone in the next life. So the body was stuffed to
plump it up like a cushion. Since the stuffing wouldn't
be seen, its composition could be anything to hand –
old rags, dried moss, sawdust or even mud. (But no
sage-and-onion has been detected. Yet.)

7   The man who performed the bowelectomy was called
the 'Ripper'. His task was considered tainted and
slightly disgusting, like that of a mediaeval hangman.
So, like the hangman, he disguised himself with a black
hood and cloak. As he entered the Beautiful House
to perform his task it was the role of the embalmers
to shout abuse and insults at him ... it was as much a
part of the game as spectators hurling abuse at referees
during a football match. The insults were probably
similar too – references to his parentage, his personal
habits and his body odour. (Probably no reference to his
needing an optician though.)

---

* Not to be confused with a poisoned puss – the cats killed to accompany
their owners into the afterlives ... or the after-nine-lives.

8   If you want a taste of holiness yourself then squeeze
the oil from pistachio nuts and rub it into your body. It
conferred divinity on the dead body. The oil, known as
senetjer, also guaranteed immortality. You, wise reader,
unlike the mummy, will rub it in BEFORE you die. You
may smell like a snack bowl in a cocktail bar, but at least
you'll outlive the mockers. (Possibly.)

9   The Beautiful House was usually erected outside the
city walls so the smells wouldn't put the poor peasants
off their porridge. The trouble was, this laid the corpses
open to attack from passing jackals fancying a pharaoh
flapjack or a salted steak from a superior scribe. When
this happened the embalmers simply replaced the missing
body-bits with wooden replicas. Ramesses II had his
nostrils stuffed with peppercorns to keep the hook shape
of his nose from collapsing. An idea not to be sneezed at.

10   This is so disgusting you really do not want to know.
All right, on your head be it. A royal princess may have
been untouchable in life, but in the Beautiful House her
beautiful body was vulnerable to abuse. Herodotus wrote
of an embalmer who confessed to the act of necrophilia
with one of his corpses. This is one step down from
flogging a dead horse, of course. The practice was
counteracted by relatives of the dead leaving a corpse
untouched for three or four days. That way, when it was
delivered to the embalmer, it would have rotted enough
to deter all but the most hardened offender.

'The difference between sex and death is that with
death you can do it alone and no one is going to make
fun of you.'

Woody Allen (1935—), American writer, director and actor

— KHUFU'S MUMMY MYSTERY —

> 'When sleep enters the body like smoke
> And man journeys into the abyss
> Like an extinguished star that is lighted elsewhere,
> Then all quarrel ceases.'
>
> *Nelly Sachs (1891–1970), Jewish German poet and playwright*

If Khufu wasn't found in the Great Pyramid then bits of his mummy were … No, not his *mummy*, his mother, Queen Hetep-Heres. Her grave was a deep pit near the Great Pyramid. It remained hidden for 3,000 years. Then a photographer set up his tripod to record some archaeological diggings. One leg of his tripod appeared to sink through solid rock. It turned out to be not sandstone but a plaster cover over a 30-metre pit. That shaft was quite an engineering feat for the ancients.

When the rubble was removed the queen's tomb was revealed. Her white coffin lay there and the excited archaeologists could scarcely wait to gaze upon the oldest mummy ever seen. Inside they found two silver bracelets.

Her mummified body was missing. Mysteriously, the canopic jars holding her embalmed viscera were intact – interesting because they were the oldest example of mummified organs in Egyptology.

How and why was she buried there? Another mystery. Perhaps her original tomb, near husband Sneferu at Dahshur, had been robbed and her mummy destroyed in the search for treasures wrapped inside the bandages. Perhaps the guards arrived in time to save the canopic jars. Her son, Khufu, may have decided she'd be safer near his own Great Pyramid at Giza.

But if damaged mummies can't function in the afterlife, what was the point in burying Mum's offal? An alternative theory is that the undertakers and the guards conspired to conceal mummy's mummy condition from Pharaoh Khufu – he was led to believe his old mater was inside that sarcophagus. No servant had the nerve to say, 'Sorry, sir, but your mum's a few joints short of a Sunday dinner.'

Did you know ... medicinal mummies

The idea of grinding up mummies to a powder and using it as a medicine was something practised in Europe in mediaeval times. Superstitious nonsense of an ignorant age, you will say.

Yet Merc Pharmaceuticals were still making Ancient Egyptian mummies into medicine as late as 1924. How many people took the powders and, unwittingly, committed cannibalism, we do not know.

Death-watch duties

'The magician and the politician have much in common: they both have to draw our attention away from what they are really doing.'

Ben Okri (1959—), Nigerian novelist

Before 1832, the only legal supply of corpses for surgeons to dissect in the UK were those of prisoners condemned to death. Courts grew kinder, dissection material became scarce and, under the immutable laws of economics, supply rose to meet demand. If you had a dead body you could sell it for a tidy sum.

If you *didn't* have a dead body to sell then you could dig one up from the local graveyard soon after it had been interred. The surgeons would slip you a fiver – no questions asked.* Families of the deceased had a couple of defences. They could either bury their loved one with a metal cage around the coffin or they could hire an armed guard to watch over the grave.†

Bodysnatching is seen as a phenomenon of the early 1800s. But Egyptians faced the same problem. NOT from the sly surgeons, but from magicians. An old Egyptian papyrus tells the tale ...

The witch-watch

Telephron was a student and, as is the way with students, he had no money. As he wandered down the main street of Larissa he saw an old man standing on a block of stone crying to passers-by, 'Does anyone want a job? A nightwatchman job. I will pay well. Does anyone want my job? Anyone?'

Telephron went up to the man and asked, 'What would you want me to guard?'

---

* The alternative was to murder some lonely person that no one would miss and sell the corpse. That was the profession of Burke and Hare in Edinburgh – on an industrial scale. They were caught eventually and Hare went free after ratting on his partner. Burke was hanged ... and dissected by the surgeons.

† Not always a safe option. The guards often needed to be fortified with strong drink. One nervous grave-watcher fired at a menacing figure, wandering in the graveyard gloom. Next morning it was revealed he had shot a passing pig.

The old man said, 'Just one dead body.'

Telephron laughed. 'Why? Do you think it might run away?'

The old man scowled at him and snapped, 'Do you know nothing, boy? There are witches all over the city. When night falls they wander the streets and seek out corpses waiting to be mummified. The witches tear off flesh from dead bodies with their teeth. They use the flesh to weave their magic spells.'

'What would I have to do?' the student asked and the old man explained:

'Stay awake all night and guard the body. If you see anything, you must drive it away. For witches can change their skins and appear as mice or birds or dogs. You must fix your eyes on my nephew's body, look neither left nor right nor even blink. If you can do that, I will pay you a thousand silver nummi.'

Telephron jumped at the offer and was then warned, 'But if the body is damaged – if there is any flesh taken from the corpse – you must replace it with a piece of your own flesh from the same place.'

And so the deal was agreed and Telephron had made the worst deal of his life …

Of course the witch arrived – in the shape of a weasel – and sent Telephron to sleep. He awoke at dawn when the funeral procession arrived. The widow examined the intact body and the student seemed to have escaped the forfeit.

A witch later confessed to the crime of stealing the corpse's nose and ears. The witch took Telephron's nose and ears to replace those of the corpse THEN made clay models to stick on the student.

Sure enough when Telephron examined them his nose crumbled in his hand and his ears fell off.

Now the story may be fiction, but the guarding of corpses was every bit as real as the Georgian bodysnatchers of 2,000 years later.

You are probably safe today because cremation turns you to ash. No one wants ashes ... except an English or Australian cricketer, of course.

— THE MUMMY PIT —

'The war against illegal plunder has been fought since the beginning of the world.'

> Frédéric Bastiat (1801–50), French economist: The Law

The Egyptians never learned. They buried their pharaohs with riches so the god-kings would live royally in the afterlife. But those riches lured every thief in the kingdom like magnets to iron filings. Instead of a heavenly afterlife, the spirits had to stagger around with ragged bodies because their mummies had been torn apart in the search for loot.

A lucky few mummified bodies were left to rest undisturbed for eternity ... or until some thoughtless archaeologist came and stuck his curious nose into the coffin.

By around 1000 BC the priests were growing weary of patching tattered pharaohs. They came up with a plan. They gathered all the mummies they could lay their hands on and hid them away in two secret caches near Thebes.

It worked ... until the archaeologists came along 3,000 years later. In the 1870s the first corpse collection of 40 pharaohs was found near Deir el-Bahari at Thebes by three local brothers. They plundered the tombs for profit for 11 years until archaeologists were led to the mummy pit and plundered it in the name of science.*

Another 16 mummies were found in the Valley of the Kings in 1898. The Valley of the Kings is situated on the West Bank of the Nile, just across from the city of Thebes, the capital of Egypt during the Middle and New Kingdoms.

This was the favourite hiding place for the tombs of the pharaohs and their royal courts at that time. The valley is located beneath a mountain that looks very much like a pyramid. It is one of the hottest, least-welcoming, quietest places on Earth.

There are some 85 tombs in the valley, ranging from simple pits to tombs with corridors, rooms and grand burial chambers. Some tombs are cut into the cliffside, others are built deep underground.

By 1890 they had all been found and excavated. Except one. Tutankhamun would have another 30 years, and a World War, to rest in peace.

Cheap and cheerless

Embalmers showed wooden models of their art to would-be buyers. The top-of-the-range mummy was up to king quality. But there were cheaper options. The process that your dear deceased went through was not something you would want to ponder on over porridge or dwell on over dinner.

There was no evisceration. There was a cheaper way of emptying the bowel cavity …

---

* Ramesses II was publicly unwrapped in 1886 in just a quarter of an hour. His body became contaminated by fungi and bacteria, which began to eat away at the corpse. In 1975, scientists used gamma rays to sterilise his body before storing it in an antibacterial case.

'Syringes are filled with oil which is then injected into the abdomen.* The passage by which it is likely to return is stopped.† The body is laid in natron salt and at the end of the prescribed time the cedar oil is allowed to escape.‡ Such is its power that it brings with it the whole stomach and intestines in liquid state.'

Herodotus

He goes on to say that once the body is dried it is returned to the relative with no further treatment. You do not get the gift-wrapping package in the cut-price option. (Maybe a trip to St John's Ambulance will finish the job with a free bandaging service.)

DYNASTIES 11–17
THE MIDDLE KINGDOM
(2181–1570 BC)

For 140 years Egypt suffered from the chaos of the First Intermediate Period (2181–2040). Tombs were looted, there were strikes and riots while, at the top, pharaohs were being assassinated by power-hungry generals or relatives.§

---

* Come on, Herodotus, stop being bashful. You mean through the rectum. It's surprising there are no records of mummies with watering eyes. Ouch.
† Let's be clear about this. The embalmer sticks a bung up the butt of the body. Or instructs his assistant, 'Put a sock in it.'
‡ Yes, the bung is removed. If you try this at home it is as well to stand clear or use a telescopic device to pop the cork. This is a champagne moment.
§ A shrunken kingdom based in Memphis saw 17 pharaohs in 20 years. Not quite up to the pace of the Roman emperors 2,000 years later, but unsettling. 'God save king … erm … who is it this month?'

Mentuhotep was the man to sort things out. ('Sort things out' is a hieroglyphic euphemism for 'kill people'.)

— MENTUHOTEP I —
(ruled 2060–2010 BC), 11th Dynasty

> 'At some future period the civilised races of man will almost certainly exterminate, and replace the savage races throughout the world.'
>
> *Charles Darwin (1809–82), British naturalist*[*]

After 14 peaceful years along came Mentuhotep's *annus horribilis* – 'Year of the crime of Thinis'. Rebels were desecrating sacred sites and Mentuhotep sent an army to confront them. He succeeded in reuniting Egypt north and south after years of division. This kicked off the era known as 'The Middle Kingdom'.

So many heroes died in Mentuhotep's battles he was obliged to invent the world's first war cemetery.

Soldiers had always been buried on the battlefield, but in the 1920s the American Egyptologist Herbert Winlock (1884–1950) found the grave of Mentuhotep. Nearby were the graves of 60 of his warriors, wrapped in linen but not mummified. They'd almost certainly been repatriated from a Nubian battlefield, hundreds of miles away. Maybe they were buried near the pharaoh so they could fight Mentuhotep's battles in the afterlife … or maybe they were just good company on a pub crawl.

---

[*] Excuse me, Mr Darwin. I know you're a genius and all that, but if the civilised races 'exterminate' the savage races then the civilised would have to be pretty savage, wouldn't they? Either a paradox, or you are talking through your intelligent hat.

Did you know ... devotion

Ancient Egypt is so far away from our digital world
it's easy to forget how much we have in common
with those fellow humans. They may have lived 4,000
years ago but some of their feelings are as fresh as
tomorrow's daisies. In 2200 BC a man named Sau (who
lived during the 12th Dynasty) made plans to be buried
in his father's mausoleum ...

'In order that I might be with him in one place. It's
not that I can't afford a second tomb, but I did this in
order that I might see my father every day.'

Poignant. Let's hope he found his dad in some paternal
paradise.

— MENTUHOTEP III —
(ruled 1997–1991 BC), 11th Dynasty

'Nobody gets justice. People only get good luck or
bad luck.'
Orson Welles (1915–85), American actor, director, writer

Justice. Getting what you deserve. Sometimes it DOES
happen, Mr Welles.

Mentuhotep III's vanity project was to send an army of
10,000 men to find a block of stone suitable for the lid of his
sarcophagus. The man he put in charge of the expedition was
his vizier, Amenemhet.

Now 10,000 men sounds a bit excessive for a simple

stone-finding expedition, but what the pharaoh wants the pharaoh gets.

Amenemhet set off and, lo, he had an omen. A pregnant gazelle led the 10,000 men to a slab of fine stone and gave birth on top of it. What a wonderful animal. How could they reward it?

They sacrificed it. (What happened to the baby Bambi, we don't know. But, with 10,000 hungry men to feed, its prospects were about those of a fish on Mars.)

The block was detached and carried back to Thebes, where Mentuhotep gloated over the gruesome and gazelle-gored granite. Then the avenging god of gazelles struck.*

A military coup, led by Amenemhet and the ready-made army of 10,000, overthrew the pharaoh.

The 11th Dynasty died with Mentuhotep. Long live the 12th Dynasty. All for Mentuhotep's vanity.

> 'I've only been in love with a beer bottle and a mirror.'†
> *Sid Vicious (1957–79), English punk rock bass guitarist and vocalist*

---

* The god of gazelles is a massively popular deity in the pantheon, appealed to constantly by those who cry, 'Deer God!'

† Mr Vicious is being economical with the truth. He also had a love of drugs. He died in his sleep in 1979, having overdosed on the heroin his mother had procured. That's what mums are for, innit.

— AMENEMHET I —
(1991–1962 BC), 12th Dynasty

> 'There is no act of treachery or meanness of which
> a political party is not capable; for in politics there
> is no honour.'
>
> *Benjamin Disraeli (1804–81), British prime minister and novelist*

Amenemhet was the first ruler of the new 12th Dynasty. He rose from the post of vizier to take the throne with the help of his gang of heavies. This strong man of politics secured the country against the Sand Dwellers – tribes in the north-east of the country who had been terrorising the trade routes.

Amenemhet lasted 30 years and brought stability to Egypt. But he was assassinated – butchered in his bed while the palace guards were absent. He had surrounded himself with ambitious men who helped him to power. It was inevitable that those ambitions would drive them to take his top spot. The only surprise is that it took them 30 years.

> 'He who, blinded by ambition, raises himself to a
> position whence he cannot mount higher, must
> thereafter fall with the greatest loss.'
>
> *Niccolò Machiavelli (1469–1527), Italian historian, diplomat*

His son, Senusret I, hurried home from a war against the Libyans to claim the throne.

⚊ SENUSRET III ⚊
(ruled 1870–1831 BC), 12th Dynasty

> 'No one had rights or a vote but the king;
> In fact you might say he was fairly right wing.'
>
> *Tim Rice (1944—), British lyricist: lyric to 'Pharaoh Story',*
> Joseph and the Amazing Technicolor Dreamcoat

This Senusret was the pharaoh who was believed to have lived in *Technicolor Dreamcoat* Joseph's day ... though Senusret wasn't named in the Bible's Book of Genesis.

The story of Joseph has been retold for thousands of years. You know it.

🕴 Joseph, his dad's favourite son, was sold into Egyptian slavery by his jealous brothers. They envied the parental gift of the blingy coat.

🕴 As a Hebrew slave, Joseph was wrongly imprisoned when he rejected the advances of his rich master's wife.

🕴 Fellow prisoners told him their dreams and he interpreted them. The pharaoh's butler, who shared his cell, was told by Joseph that he'd be restored to the pharaoh's favour in three days ...

🕴 ... and lo, it came to pass. Joseph told an imprisoned baker that *his* dream meant he'd be hanged in three days – and lo, that came to pass too. (Is that the sort of prediction *you'd* like to hear as you read your horoscope over your cornflakes? Probably not.)

🕴 The ungrateful butler forgot Joseph's help until ...

'In his bed Pharaoh had an uneasy night
He had had a dream that pinned him to his sheets
    with fright.
No one knew the meaning of this dream
What to do, whatever could it mean?
Then his butler said, "I know of a bloke in jail
Who is hot on dreams."

'Poor, Poor Pharaoh',
Joseph and the Amazing Technicolor Dreamcoat

Joseph interpreted the pharaoh's dream, saved Egypt from a famine and became a top adviser to the pharaoh.

When the drought struck the whole of the Middle East, Joseph's brothers arrived in Egypt hoping to buy grain for their family.

Joseph, the pharaoh's right-hand man, gave them a hard time but in the end he and his family were reconciled.

Happy ever after; a Cinderella riches-to-rags-to-riches story. Joseph lived to a ripe old 110 years, was mummified and taken back to his homeland for burial.

It would be a wonderful tale if it were only true.* The whole thing is probably a fiction that became accepted as history. If a story makes a successful musical then it's probably a myth.

So if Joseph is a fiction, what about Moses and the great Jewish Exodus from Egypt?

---

* I am on dangerous ground here, arguing with God's holy word. There is every chance she may strike me down with a thunderbolt. It's a risk writers have to take. If this book ends with a scorched page and the smell of smoking flesh, you'll know what happened.

The Moses Myth

The traditional story says Joseph died and another famine hit Egypt. Joseph's Jewish people in Egypt were seen as a threat, so were rounded up to serve as slaves. When their numbers grew to two million the pharaoh worried the Jewish slaves would ally with Egypt's enemies and the country would be destroyed from within and without.

The pharaoh ordered the killing of all Hebrew boys, but baby Moses escaped when he was placed in a basket and hidden among reeds at the edge of the Nile. The pharaoh's daughter found him and raised him in the royal court.*

Moses demanded the Jews be set free – or else. When the pharaoh refused the Egyptians were hit with ten plagues ... including the river turning to blood, a plague of frogs, flood, drought, famine, disease, flies, gnats, locusts and darkness. The pharaoh didn't take the hint so God wiped out all the Egyptians' first-born sons.† That did the trick.

The pharaoh was now begging Moses to lead the Jewish people out of Egypt with their livestock and go off to the Promised Land, which they did.

In an added plot-twist the pharaoh changed his mind and chased after them with an army. When he caught them at the Red Sea the waters parted to allow the Jews

---

* The story has the mythical feel of Romulus and Remus, abandoned at birth before growing up to found Rome. Was the Moses basket just a reworking of a really ancient tale? King Sargon the Great of Mesopotamia (ruled 22nd and 23rd centuries BC) was said to have been laid in a basket and put in the river as a baby.

† The death of the first-born is called Passover because the Angel of Death 'passed over' the Jewish children and only killed the Egyptian boys.

to escape. When the Egyptians tried to follow, the waves returned to swallow them.*

The Jews were favoured by God – the 'Chosen People' – and in return they'd worship Him alone ... and make a blood sacrifice: the foreskin of every male child. They also agreed to stick to the Ten Commandments that God handed to Moses on tablets of stone.

It's a story as dramatic as Joseph's but the flight from Egypt, the Exodus, is increasingly doubted as 'fact' because ...

- There is no archaeological evidence, despite rigorous searches. You'd think millions of people living in a desert for 40 years would leave some trace.

- There is no record of a mass emigration in Egyptian writings. There is no grave epitaph that records a victim's death from one of the plagues.†

- The logistics are hard to believe (unless God intervened); 600,000 Jewish men with their families and animals marching ten abreast would have formed a convoy 150 miles long, all to be fed as they crossed the Sinai desert.

- Moses was 80 when he made his demands of the pharaoh – the same pharaoh who had ordered the killing of Israelite boys 80 years before. So how old was the pharaoh?‡

---

* This was depicted in Cecil B. DeMille's *The Ten Commandments* movie using sea-coloured jelly, sliced in half and shaken to replicate waves – which is a trifle cheap. We don't know how God managed the original.
† For example, an epitaph reading, 'Here lies Set – sleeps like a dog; in his throat they found a frog.' Or, 'Here lies Tuthmose, killed like a rat; Bitten by a septic gnat.'
‡ Of course Moses himself was said to have died on his 120th birthday. That must have put a bit of a damper on the birthday party. The old guy should have kept taking the tablets.

So it seems some of Egypt's greatest stories are just fictions.

There *is* a historical pharaoh, Akhenaten, who enforced the worship of the sun god Aten. That was deeply unpopular and when he died an Egyptian inscription records that the angry old gods threatened Egypt with plagues if they weren't worshipped again – and those plagues sound familiar:

- 𓂀 Hapi, god of the Nile, would make its waters undrinkable;

- 𓂀 Kermit,* the goddess of fertility, would release frogspawn to swarm over the land;

- 𓂀 Osiris, the god of corn, would allow locusts to devour Egypt's crops;

- 𓂀 Ra, the sun god, would refuse to shine.

Maybe the Israelites adapted this snippet of Egyptian conflict to be part of their own story – a story told to explain why they were the chosen people, and why they were entitled to move in to their promised land. First came the action, then the justification was adopted ... 'We were persecuted in Egypt, so God insisted we colonise this land.'

> 'An explanation of cause is not a justification by reason.'
> *C. S. Lewis (1898–1963), British author and theologian*

Nubian nastiness

Whatever the truth of the Exodus, Senusret III was a ruthless warrior. The Nubians on the southern borders of Egypt were a constant thorn in the side of the pharaohs. Senusret

---

* No I did not make that up.

III dredged the Nile so his warships could sail far south and strike at the heart of the Nubian lands. He built fortified granaries so there was a secure supply line for his army. The punishment of Nubia was planned as meticulously as D-Day. The Nubians had no chance.

Senusret III recorded his own version of his victory, so we can expect a little exaggeration ...

> 'I captured their women, I carried off their subjects, went forth to their wells, smote their bulls, I reaped their grain and set fire thereto. I speak in truth.'
>
> *Senusret III, 1862 BC*

Methinks the pharaoh doth protest too much. An exaggeration or a lie? If he's a liar, he's in good company ...

> 'Actors are good liars; writers are good liars with good memories.'
>
> *Daniel Keys Moran (1962—), US science-fiction writer*

Senusret III knew that one day he'd become a god and his fighting days would be over. He didn't want to see his gains reversed. So he left behind him a warning to his successors – a threat from the grave:

> 'To every son of mine who keeps my borders. He is my son, born of my person. But if he abandon the boundary, if he will not fight for it, he is no son of mine and was not born of me.'

And to reinforce his demands he had his own statue erected there to remind heirs and enemies alike.

> 'My person has had a statue of My Person set up on
> the boundary that my person has made, so that you
> might be inspired by it and fight for it.'*

Senusret III made such an impression during his Nubian
conquest the victims eventually adopted him as their god.

BRIEF TIMELINE

THE POWER OF THE PEOPLE

2181 BC Egypt splits into rival dynasties based in Herakleopolis
and Thebes. This First Intermediate Period will
see Egypt divided for 120 years then the Middle
Kingdom begins. Death is democratised – the
afterlife is for everyone, not just kings.

1991 BC Egyptians have a 24-sign alphabet.

1720 BC Enemies from Hyksos sack Memphis.

1663 BC Hyksos rules North and Thebans the south.

---

* Senusret III's statues were placed all over Egypt to remind his people
who was in charge. They wore a grim expression, designed to express his
ruthless policies. They were unusually lifelike except for the enlarged ears
– a symbol of the fact that the king hears everything. Elizabeth I had a
portrait in which she wears a gown decorated with embroidered ears to
give the same message: mighty monarchs have Big Ears ... but Noddy
escaped.

— TAO I —
(ruled *c.* 1560 BC), 17th Dynasty

Egypt was about to be invaded by a new enemy ...

> 'By main force they easily seized Egypt without striking a blow; and having overpowered the rulers of the land, they then burned our cities ruthlessly, razed to the ground the temples of gods. Finally, they appointed one of their number as king.'
>
> *Josephus (AD 37–100), Romano-Jewish historian*

It wasn't only the Nubians to the south who looked at Egypt's riches with greed in their hearts. Around 1582 BC the Hyksos people from Asia arrived in Egypt and took over the north. Their ruling families formed the 15th and 16th Dynasties, while the 17th Dynasty of native Egyptians evolved in the south. They would come to blows.

Modern historians say Egypt was probably weakened by famines and plagues and the Hyksos walked in through an open door – hence Josephus's 'seized Egypt without striking a blow'.

The Egyptians went on ruling in the south – maybe as vassals to the Hyksos. If the Hyksos were all-conquering it was because they had a novel way of fighting – they rode on chariots. The Egyptians had never encountered such efficient war machinery before. The Hyksos used powerful composite bows and improved arrows. Their battle-axes were better than the Egyptians', they wore mail coats and they built better fortifications.

They brought a new culture to Egypt that included horse burials, new crops and new animals. The Egyptians seemed to loathe their cuckoo neighbours and in time the worm turned.

The Hyksos pharaoh in the north, Apepi (1575–1540 BC, 15th Dynasty), sent a bizarre and provocative message to the Egyptian pharaoh, Tao, in the south …

> 'I am angry, Tao. I cannot rest in my bed in Avaris because I am disturbed by the roaring of your hippos at Thebes. I want you to do something about this immediately or I shall take action.'

Yes, it's nasty to be kept awake by your neighbour's roaring hippos. But Apepi's palace was 500 miles from Tao's hippos in Thebes. There was only one answer Tao could make to that sort of bullying. Defiance. Tao replied to the effect, 'Come on then. Let's be having you, Apepi.' Tao was not nicknamed 'Tao the Brave' for nothing.

In the resulting battles the Hyksos were eventually driven out. Their monuments were destroyed. They were erased from Egyptian history as if they'd never existed.

> 'Syme was not only dead, he was abolished, an unperson.'
>
> George Orwell (1903–50), English author: 1984

But Tao probably didn't enjoy the victory. His mummy was discovered at Deir el-Bahari in 1881. When unwrapped, his skull showed damage from a mace blow, a spear stab, a dagger cut and an axe hack. He was mummified so quickly the blood had not been washed from his hair.

The blows were all to one side of the head, as if he'd been knocked down and finished off … or was lying asleep on his side when he was assassinated. The latest theory is he was executed by the Hyksos after being captured on the battlefield.

We just don't know – and Tao isn't talking. (The axe-blow fractured his jaw.)

Did you know ... parasitic punishment

Speaking of worms turning ...

Examination of mummies has shown that parasites such as worms were a problem for the Egyptians. The guinea worm would grow into a three-foot-long worm inside the body and then exit through the skin after a year. Painful.

EMPIRE BUILDERS

— THE MASTER MYTH —

> 'It is for the good of the state that men should be deluded by religion.'
>
> *Publius Papinius Statius (AD 45–96), Roman poet*

Myths matter. One myth in particular shaped Egyptian thinking for thousands of years. And one master-myth can take the credit for leaving us a million mummies to study...

The Osiris myth

Osiris was said to be the ruler of the underworld, and his wife was Isis, a mother goddess among many other things. He had a brother, Set, who was jealous of his popularity.*

---

* Hints of Joseph and his coat of many colours, don't you think?

The plot was ingenious. First Set took Osiris's measurements and had a coffin made to be a perfect fit. The sneaky sibling, Set, organised a feast and invited Osiris.* With the party in full swing, Set produced the casket and said that it would be given to whoever it fitted. All the guests tried but only Osiris fitted.

Set slammed the lid down and sealed the casket shut with molten lead. The coffin was then thrown into the Nile.

Isis was distraught and searched Egypt then overseas. She eventually found where the coffin had come to rest in the roots of a massive tree.

Isis returned the coffin to Egypt for a proper burial. For safekeeping she hid it in the marshes beside the Nile. Of course the wicked Set found the casket while he was out hunting. The savage sibling Set set upon the body of Osiris and sliced it into 13 pieces. He scattered the parts throughout the land of Egypt.

Now Isis had to set out again, looking for the parts of her husband. Eventually she found all the parts – except his penis – assembled him like a 3D jigsaw and wrapped him in bandages to keep the bits together. (The penis was eaten by a catfish and never seen again.)

In some accounts Isis breathed life back into Osiris's body and it was then that Horus was conceived.†

The young Horus went out to battle against his Uncle Set, determined to avenge his father's death.

---

* You could say it was a Set-up. But I wouldn't dream of it.

† Of course you can spot the fatal flaw in that story. Considering the one part of Osiris that Isis couldn't find, it was a miraculous conception. Some versions suggest Isis conceived Horus *before* Osiris was jig-sawed, and that makes more sense … if indeed we are looking for 'sense' in a myth.

After a series of fights, detailed in 'The battles of Horus and Set', neither god was able to secure an outright victory. So it was a draw. Osiris was declared king of the underworld, Horus king of the living, and Set ruler of the deserts as the god of chaos and evil.

Horus the sun rules the days while Set the darkness takes over at night.

You'll appreciate that the wrapping of the mummy is in imitation of Osiris and his butchery. Stay in one piece and you can enter the afterlife … give or take a catfish nibble.

There are many variations of the story and echoes of myths from the dawn of time … Set, on hearing of the birth of Horus, plotted to kill the baby. Was that tale later plagiarised to become the story about King Herod and baby Jesus?

— SOOTHING — SUPERSTITIONS

So you think that being mauled by a crocodile is a fate to be avoided?

You must be forgetting that it is in fact an honour, and that your relatives will find consolation in your end … if they can find an 'end' after you've been through the blender of crocodile teeth. Once your remains are washed up, you will be treated with religious respect – a sacrificial victim to the crocodile god.

> 'Whenever anyone (Egyptian or foreigner) has lost his
> life by falling prey to a crocodile, or by drowning in
> the river, the law compels the inhabitants of the
> nearest city to have them embalmed. The remains
> will be buried in a sacred place with all magnificence.
> No one may touch the corpse, not even the friends or
> relatives. Only the priests of the Nile who prepare it
> for burial with their own hands may touch it and
> treat it as more than the body of a man. They alone
> shall lay it in the tomb.'
>
> *Herodotus*

What more can you ask? You are indeed honoured to have
been crunched by a crocodile. On the other hand, your
relatives can't touch your mangled, crushed, mauled and
disfigured remains. No slobbering sister or mourning
mother to kiss your corpse. So every silver lining has a cloud.

Did you know ... the Creation

The sun god Atum was the first being. He created two
more gods from his own semen, by his own hand.
Priestesses in his temple at Karnak re-enacted this
event using a phallic statue – only without the same
outcome, obviously.

Victorian museum curators locked away such
'abominable monuments to human licentiousness'.
Rumour has it these phallic collections were added to
when the curators broke off bits from classical statues.
This served a double function of cleaning up the spicy
statues and adding to their secret stores. Two birds
with one stone phallus.

THE NEW KINGDOM
DYNASTIES 18–20
(1570–1070)

The Egyptians hated the Hyksos interlopers who ruled Lower Egypt and the Nile Delta. A new kingdom and a new era was about to dawn. Egypt and her pharaoh-gods would be great once again. But first they had to rid themselves of the ruling trespassers from the northern Delta.

⟶ APEPI THE SNAKE ⟵
(ruled 1575–1540 BC), 15th Dynasty

> 'Let a man then know his worth, and keep things under his feet. Let him not peep or steal, or skulk up and down with the air of a charity-boy, a bastard, or an interloper.'
>
> *Ralph Waldo Emerson (1803–82), American essayist and poet*

Apepi has had a bad press. He was one of the last of the interlopers and must have felt their power draining away as the native Egyptians in the Upper Kingdom fought back. He defeated the head-crushed Tao I, but it turned out to be a hollow victory. Tao's successor was even more aggressive.

Apepi behaved like a true cuckoo in the Egyptian nest. He didn't build many monuments – he simply attached his name to the existing statues and sphinxes that he came across. He looted the temples and tombs he found.

For the first 20 years of his reign this last great Hyksos ruler had created a vibrant state. Then the Egyptians of the south destroyed the peace and turned Apepi into a warrior king – one who made vainglorious boasts. On his monuments he braggingly said of himself …

> He whose power brings about victorious frontiers
> One to whom every country must pay tribute
> Stout-hearted on the battlefield
> Great is his strength

Wishful thinking. Great *had been* his strength … till old age came calling and death claimed the 60-plus-year-old.

Apepi shared his name with the Egyptians' mythical snake of chaos and was reviled as such. The good things he did have been forgotten.

> 'The evil that men do lives after them; the good is oft interred with their bones.'
>
> *William Shakespeare*: Julius Caesar

Too true, Will, too true.

His successor lasted barely a year before the hated Hyksos were harried out of the land.

The Admirable Ahmose

Admiral Ahmose was in at the kill when the Hyksos finally fell. He fought hand-to-hand at a naval battle and his reward was to be given the hand of a dead enemy.

No sooner were the Hyksos dispatched than Ahmose was sent to suppress rebels in the South. He was rewarded with prisoners of war as slaves ... which are more useful than dead hands. Handier, in fact.

Nubian invaders tried to take advantage of the civil war in Egypt but were defeated. Ahmose fought under three kings in ten campaigns. He was one of the soldier/sailor heroes who would bring back stability to Egypt during the 18th Dynasty.

— HATSHEPSUT —
(1479–1458 BC), 18th Dynasty

> 'No doubt exists that all women are crazy; it's only a question of degree.'
>
> *W.C. Fields (1880–1946) American actor*

Pharaoh Tuthmose I (1506–1493 BC) had a short but spectacular reign. He was not a member of the royal family but a military veteran who married into it and took over the throne in middle age. Using all that army training he attacked the Nubians to the south to stop their incursions. Like many pharaohs he was seen to lead from the front – and you wouldn't want to stand in his way. A chronicle says ...

> 'His majesty Tuthmose I was a furious threat, like a panther. His majesty cast the first lance, which remained in the body of the fallen one. In an instant of destruction their people were brought off as living prisoners. His majesty sailed down-river with that wretched Nubian troglodyte general hanging head downwards at the prow of his barge.'

He had a daughter, Hatshepsut – a name meaning 'Foremost of noblewomen'. She planned to live up to her name.

When Tuthmose I died, his throne passed to his son, Tuthmose II (1493–1479 BC), who proved every bit as ruthless as Dad.

He led an army to deal with the troublesome Kush and was not above a little genocide ... in the name of peace, of course. It always is.

> 'This army of Tuthmose II overthrew those barbarians. They did not let live anyone among their males. Except one of those sons of the chief of the wretched Kush. He was taken away as a prisoner.'
>
> *Anonymous report (1518 BC)*

'Those barbarians' were innocent children, slaughtered so Egypt could keep a secure border. Butchering Tuthmose II carelessly died in his early thirties and left the succession in limbo. The young Pharaoh Tuthmose III was the nominal ruler, but he was a child when his father Tuthmose II died.

Who better to help you rule than your ruthless and ambitious stepmother, Hatshepsut?

> 'His sister and wife, Hatshepsut, controlled the affairs of the land.'
>
> *Tomb inscription*

But once the reins were in her hands it was going to prove tough to prise them free. In the annals of pharaohs, Hatshepsut was to be one of the really odd ones. For a start, she was a female pharaoh. The Egyptians were all for royal lines descending through queens, but didn't usually have one on the throne ... though there had been precedents.

Hatshepsut had been married to her half-brother, Tuthmose II, so she was also the young king's auntie. Confused? Imagine how Tuthmose III must have felt.

She began a propaganda campaign – like a political poster campaign carved in rock reliefs. Of all the world's modern political slogans, one is maybe more apt than the rest:

> 'They can't lick our Dick.'
>
> *Unofficial poster campaign for Richard Nixon (1972)*

Her spin-doctoring suggested that she was fathered by the god Amun to rule Egypt and her images are decorated with the official royal false beard. She also created the myth that her much-loved earthly father, Tuthmose I, had overseen her coronation before he died. All a tall story to create her own legend.

She was at first the power behind the throne. But Hatshepsut could not have assumed power without a team of powerful officials. Behind every great woman there is a man giving her a leg-up. For Hatshepsut it was her steward, Senenmut.

He has more statues dedicated to him than any other official in the history of Egypt – the gifts of Hatshepsut to her loyal henchman.

Yet when Hatshepsut decided to assume full powers as pharaoh, Senenmut's status slipped. Why? Had he served his usefulness? Was he cast aside like a worn-out sandal?

He had two funerary monuments constructed, but they were never occupied. He vanished off the radar of Egyptian history. His reputation was trashed and traduced by jealous enemies. Once he lost Hatshepsut's patronage he was doomed to be defamed, disparaged and denigrated.

> 'I don't like country music, but I don't mean to
> denigrate those who do. And for the people who like
> country music, denigrate means "put down".'
>
> *Bob Newhart (1929—), American stand-up comedian*

Senenmut never married. Was he Hatshepsut's lover? Was that the secret of his rise and fall? The plaything of a ruthless woman, rejected when she grew bored with him? We'll probably never know. What a story it would make.*

Hatshepsut ruled successfully for over 20 years but in the meantime young Tuthmose III had grown into a man with a mind of his own. After 20 years he was probably tired of waiting to rule in his own right, so it seems likely he indulged in a little step-matricide and sent her to an early sarcophagus. It's always been a dangerous business being a regent – rivals want your influence and the king-in-waiting doesn't wait forever.

BRIEF TIMELINE

DECLINE AND FALL

1570 BC	Foreign rulers, the Hyksos, thrown out and the 'New Kingdom' begins.
1540 BC	Egyptians switch from building pyramids for their pharaoh to burying them in tombs cut into rock.
1450 BC	The kings start using a new title: pharaoh.

* Senenmut vanished from the records so completely there is no trace of his death. So readers inclined to melodrama may like to think it was some noir murder plot – that Hatshepsut had him sent to the Big Sleep. 'It's the Long Goodbye for you, Senenmut. Farewell My Lovely.' (A reputable historian would never dream of suggesting such a thing.)

1275 BC   Battle of Kadesh and (possible) exodus of the
          Jews.

1070–712 BC   Collapse of the New Kingdom.

⌐ TUTHMOSE III ⌐
(1479–1425 BC), 18th Dynasty

'God placed me on the throne, and you reptiles of the
earth dare oppose me. I render an account of my
government to none save God.'

Napoleon Bonaparte (1769–1821), French military and political leader

This 21-year-old Mr Angry turned his testosterone-
driven rage on Egypt's enemies. The strategy was to attack
neighbouring states and create a military buffer zone. Those
neighbours had been getting a bit above themselves while
Hatshepsut had ruled. Now it was payback time.

Tuthmose III was an enthusiastic hunter. It was claimed
he killed a whole herd of elephants in a single morning.
(Strange that it took him 21 years to kill one stepmother
then.) One of his officers boasted …

'In Syria Tuthmose III hunted 120 elephants for the
sake of their tusks. I engaged the largest of them,
which was clashing with his majesty. I cut off its
trunk while it was still alive. My lord rewarded me
with gold and three changes of clothing.'

Amenemhab, army officer (1471 BC)

Nowadays he, and his exterminating boss, would be rewarded with a lengthy prison sentence.

Elephants weren't Tuthmose III's only target. He also seemed determined to erase stepmummy Hatshepsut's *name* from the history of the nation. For decades Egyptologists have been saying the young pharaoh's rage at his stepmother was expressed in the way he had her name erased from the list of kings and destroyed many of her monuments.* He must have enjoyed that. There is also a hint that she murdered Tuthmose's dad, Tuthmose II, her husband and half-brother.† If someone turned your daddy into a mummy, then you'd probably be vengeful too.

But modern historians point out that ...

🛆 the monuments weren't damaged or hidden until 20 years after Hatshepsut died – hardly a case of dancing on stepmother's freshly filled grave;

🛆 Hatshepsut isn't the only pharaoh to have suffered that post-mortem indignity. It was merely a political ploy to stop Hatshepsut's relatives claiming her inheritance – Tuthmose wanted the throne to pass peacefully to his son.

Whatever the truth, a new and virile pharaoh took the throne and the Middle East was about to be shaken. Tuthmose would take part in 17 campaigns and expand Egypt's lands to the most extensive ever – from Syria in the north to

---

* Some were simply walled up out of sight. Ironically, this preserved them for posterity, so instead of being forgotten, as he intended, she is well remembered.

† Since Tuthmose II was a god, her crimes were 'deicide', as well as fratricide, matricide and good old homicide.

Nubia in the south. He earned himself the modern epithet, 'the Napoleon of Egypt'.*

Typical Tuth tactic

> 'Let your plans be dark and as impenetrable as night, and when you move, fall like a thunderbolt.'
>
> *Sun Tzu (544–496 BC), Chinese military strategist*

Tuthmose marched at the head of his troops, mopping up town after town on his way to a prime target, Megiddo. Tuthmose's spies said the city was hosting a meeting of anti-Egypt allies.

> 'The capture of Megiddo is the capture of a thousand towns.'
>
> *Tuthmose III: campaign annals on walls of Karnak Temple*

A rebellious Canaanite prince was lurking there and Tuthmose wanted to make an example of him.

There were three routes to the city – two easy, and one through a narrow pass where his army could only proceed in single file. His generals pointed out that the narrow pass was potentially suicidal – a rebel ambush would be almost certain to succeed. Tuthmose chose to attack through the pass. What? Was he mad? Or was there method in such madness?

---

* A title bestowed on Tuthmose by US Egyptologist James Henry Breasted (1865–1935). Tuthmose's mummy indicates he was 5 foot 3.5 inches tall so he could have played little Napoleon in the movie of *War and Peace* … if he hadn't been mummified, obviously. However, Tuthmose never met his Waterloo, nor was he Wellington-booted into exile.

'I will proceed along this narrow road. You take the other roads if you wish. Those who would rather follow my majesty may come with me. Do we want our enemies to say, "Tuthmose has taken the easy road. He must be afraid of us"? That's what they'll say.'

Tuthmose III's address to his generals,
as reported by Thanuny, military scribe (1481 BC)

His generals, yes-men to a man, agreed. Tuthmose led the way.

When Tuthmose's Egyptians emerged they found the pass undefended – the Canaanites hadn't anticipated he'd be so rash as to take that route. It was a massive gamble, but one that paid off handsomely. Almost.

The Megiddo men were routed on the battlefield but the Egyptian army suffered a severe bout of indiscipline. Rather than follow up the victory, they started looting the surrounding area. The rebels were able to retreat to Megiddo and close the gates.

There is a delightful description of the late-coming defenders finding the gates shut against them. They were forced to scramble up the walls of their own city with help from friends who dragged them up with improvised ropes made from their clothing tied together. That bit of inventiveness even served to lift their precious war chariots to safety.

The Egyptian failure to land the knockout blow meant they were obliged to sit out a siege for seven months. So Tuthmose wasn't infallible.*

---

* And his chroniclers weren't that reliable either. The narrow pass still exists so we can see that it isn't quite so narrow and treacherous as Tuthmose claimed.

Did you know … horse sense

Tuthmose wasn't the only one to employ underhand tactics to win. In Kadesh in 1662 BC Tuthmose's enemies sent a mare onto the battlefield in order to distract and excite the Egyptian stallions so they'd be unmanageable. Tuthmose's loyal officer Amenemhab wrote …

'I pursued her on foot and with my sword I ripped open her belly; I cut off her tail and set it before the pharaoh.'

The mare wouldn't be doing a lot of exciting after that. And Tuthmose III would have been disowned as a patron of the Egyptian RSPCA.

Egypt was a rich and fairly peaceful empire once Tuthmose had squashed rebels and conquered neighbours. He was one of Egypt's greatest warrior-kings and was revered for another 1,500 years.

Of course Tuthmose III had a rich and peaceful burial. His tomb was cut into a rockface in the Valley of the Kings. When it was finished the architects demolished the steps so no one could get in and rob it.

That was a tactic as sound as a Tuthmose battle plan. Except it didn't work. It was robbed in two shakes of a giraffe-tail fly-swatter.

The mummy was found in 1881 and unwrapped in 1886. Those Egyptian statues make the pharaohs look so god-like, yet Gaston Maspero (who unwrapped Tuthmose III) argued that the pharaohs weren't all they were sculpted out to be.

Queen Elizabeth I famously had to have her withered and worn face portrayed as a fresh-faced beauty. The pharaohs had been doing the same thousands of years before. Maspero said of Tuthmose's unwrapped mummy ...

> 'His statues, though not representing him as a type of manly beauty, yet give him refined, intelligent features. But a comparison with the mummy shows that the artists have idealised their model. The forehead is abnormally low, the eyes deeply sunk, the jaw heavy, the lips thick, and the cheekbones extremely prominent; nevertheless it gave a great show of energy.'
>
> *Gaston Maspero (1846–1916), French Egyptologist*

But if you were an ancient sculptor you'd make your pharaoh look good, wouldn't you?

> 'One may define flattery as a base companionship which is most advantageous to the flatterer.'
>
> *Theophrastus (371–287 BC), Greek philosopher*

⟶ AMENHOTEP II ⟵
(1453–1419), 18th Dynasty

> 'This is a ruthless world and one must be ruthless to cope with it.'
>
> *Charlie Chaplin (1889–1977), English comic actor**

---

* An expert in ruthlessness. Like Dickens, Chaplin had his childhood cut short by poverty, forcing him to grow up quickly and fight the world to avoid going under.

Like father like son. When he was alive, Tuthmose III was pretty ruthless. His son Amenhotep II showed the same sadism. In his 1425 BC battles against the Nubians he captured seven enemy princes and wanted them killed as sacrifices to the gods. A hard day's work for the executioner, you'd think. But no. Amenhotep II insisted that he kill the princes himself. He smashed their heads with his mace.

> 'He slew with his own hand the seven princes and placed them head downwards on the prow of the royal barge. They were taken and hanged from the walls of Thebes.'
>
> *Anonymous, 1451 BC*

All pharaohs relied on administrators to do the real work, just as modern governments need civil servants. Usually these people are faceless and anonymous until they have served 30 years and get a knighthood.* But Amenhotep II's top civil servant, Qenamun, had no intention of going unnoticed. The steward to Pharaoh Amenhotep II accrued no less than 80 titles during his lifetime of devoted service. They included …

 Fan-bearer to the Lord of Two Lands

 Dearly Beloved Companion

 Master of Secrets

 Captain of Bowmen

---

* It's not clear why a civil servant would get a knighthood for doing a well-paid, risk-averse job when a self-employed cab-driver or candlestick-maker doesn't. Was Sir Galahad a pen-pusher? No. (Well, probably not.) Was Sir Francis Drake a tea-drinking, bun-eating bureaucrat? No. (Again, probably not.) The pen really is mightier than the sword that descends on the knighted shoulder.

🪲 Head of Stables

🪲 Overseer of All Kinds Of Work

... and, not the most modest of titles:

🪲 God's Father

Perhaps, as the humble son of a palace nurse, he felt the need to exaggerate his status with such titles. After all ...

> 'Bureaucracy is a giant mechanism operated by pygmies.'
>
> *Honoré de Balzac (1799–1850), French novelist*

Many of Qenamun's self-promoting titles were defaced in his tomb. Not even God's Father could deal with the jealousy of ordinary mortals.

⚊ AMENHOTEP III ⚊
(1386–1349 BC), 18th Dynasty

The next pharaoh, Amenhotep III, brought with him an era of peace and stability.

He took the throne at the age of 12 and enjoyed his hobby of hunting. The wildlife of Egypt enjoyed it less. In a single day's hunting, 170 bulls were killed of which 56 died at the hands (and spears) of Amenhotep III himself. He went out after a four-day rest and killed another 40. In his first ten years on the throne he killed 102 lions and was happy to boast about it.

The only major problem was in Nubia (again). Amenhotep's son followed the fine family tradition of butchery on an industrial scale. Hands were lopped off corpses in order to aid the counting of the dead. The 'living heads' were captives ...

> 'List of captives taken by his majesty at Ibhet:
> 150 negroes, 150 archers, 250 negresses, 55 servants,
> their children 175. Total 740 living heads.
> 312 hands of the dead.
> Total 1052.'
>
> *Anonymous papyrus (1381 BC)*

This was all accomplished in an hour. So that's a speedy 312 lives per hour, or five a minute, or one every 12 seconds. Impressive. You've got to hand it to them.

But Nubia was rich in gold mines and Egypt profited from the defeat of the old enemy. That was just as well because Amenhotep married a couple of foreign princesses and one of them brought an entourage of 317 women – a lot of mouths to feed.

His first and principal queen was Tiye – a commoner by birth – who adapted to court life like a Nile hippo to mud. She was a leader of Egyptian fashion, at least among those who could afford to dress in style. One of her more exotic creations was a feather dress with vulture wings that wrapped around her thighs. Was she tickled pink by the gown?*

The pharaoh himself was not far behind in the fashion stakes. He celebrated his 36th anniversary on the throne dressed from head to toe in gold and jewellery. There wouldn't be a 37th. Like a moderate batsman in cricket he was 50 and out.

Widow Tiye survived him by ten years, still worshipped by her family. Her grandson was buried with a lock of her

---

* The mythical mother-god of Egypt, Mut, was often depicted as a vulture. Tiye was playing at being Mut incarnate. Maybe she even believed her own publicity. We don't know Goddess Mut's views on one of her sacred and revered vultures being murdered to make a fancy dress.

hair. The grandson's name was Tutankhamun. But more of him later.

— AKHENATEN —
(1350–1334 BC), 18th Dynasty

> 'God made everything out of nothing, but sometimes the nothingness shows through.'
>
> *Paul Valéry (1871–1945) French poet*

Akhenaten wasn't Egypt's greatest pharaoh, but he was one of the more unforgettable.

He was both physically and emotionally different. His grave was discovered in 1880 and portraits of the royal couple misled the archaeologists into believing they were looking at images of two women. Akhenaten was androgynous in appearance.

He may have had Fröhlich's syndrome as the result of a tumour of the pituitary gland. He had a skull malformation, a lantern jaw and an over-large head on a long neck. He also had fatty deposits on the thighs, buttocks and breasts, which explains the archaeologists' confusion.

As for his emotional condition, he felt driven to reinvent Egyptian religion. He insisted on the worship of the sun and its disc – the Aten. It upset the priests of the old Amun – you'd expect that. Temples of Amun were closed, priesthoods disbanded, old monuments defaced.

The pharaoh built a new capital city at Armana as a focus for the worship of Aten. Why? Because the sun god, Aten, told him to do it. Akhenaten clearly had a direct line to the Sun … a hotline, some might say.

It was a religious revolution every bit as disruptive as Henry VIII's reformation in Tudor England.

The worship of Aten was never popular with the people of Egypt. They reverted to the old religions as soon as Akhenaten died, and his successor referred to the fanatical pharaoh as 'the enemy'. The new city of Armana was abandoned as a ghost town when Akhenaten died and is better preserved than most. Archaeologists have uncovered features such as a balcony where the god's representative on Earth (Akhenaten) could appear before the public – so the Vatican didn't invent that idea.

In later years the pharaoh's fervour grew. There was to be just one god in Egypt – Aten, the Sun. Monuments and engraved references to all other gods were defaced.

The zealous pharaoh wasn't even going to be diverted by his beautiful wife, Nefertiti. When it came to building Armana, he said …

> 'Nor shall the king's great wife say to me, "Look – there is a fine place for Aten's temple somewhere else." Nor shall I listen to her.'*

Aten, the one true god, died with Akhenaten. Nefertiti was a powerful and determined woman, but she was too closely linked to the despised sun god.† She was blown out from history like a candle in the wind.

---

* A bit of a recipe for a divorce there. Maybe she took him for better or for worse. But he turned out worse than she took him for.

† She gave Akhenaten no heirs to his throne, only daughters. But a secondary wife, Kya, gave the pharaoh a son, Tutankhamun. Kya fell from grace … though there are people who believe she didn't so much 'fall' as was pushed. Pushed by the controlling and ruthless Nefertiti.

The end of the era

The throne passed, like the wind, to young Tutankhamun, who quickly reversed the official religion to Amun. When young Tut died his elderly uncle Ay took the throne for three years (1325–1321 BC) and was succeeded by Horemheb (1321–1293), an army commander. He was a steely autocrat who brought in an era of strict rule.

> 'I aim to crush evil and destroy iniquity. I shall be a ruler zealous and watchful against greedy men.'
>
> *Pharaoh Horemheb: Edict*

Some of his 'watchful' new laws were harsh but fair – judges guilty of corruption would be executed. Others were the result of a lifetime's experience – the royal bodyguards were to be well rewarded; there'd be no backstabbing in Horemheb's court.

Horemheb restored stability to Egypt in his 30-year rule but died without an heir. The throne passed to his vizier, Ramesses I, and a whole new dynasty began.

Ramesses enjoyed it for two whole years (1293–1291 BC) before he popped his clogs.

The 200-year Ramesside Dynasty wouldn't simply change the face of Egypt, the new line of pharaohs would redraw the map of the Middle East. Dangerous days were about to dawn for neighbours of the Nile kings.

— RAMESSES II THE GREAT —
(1279–1212), 19th Dynasty

> 'Name me an emperor who was ever struck by
> a cannonball.'
>
> *King Charles V (1500–58), Spanish King, Holy Roman Emperor*

Ramesses was great. His monuments tell us that. How do
you get to be honoured with the 'Great' label? Like Alfred
the Great in England, you could win lots of battles.* And
as Ramesses II sired 50 sons and 53 daughters he was clearly
up to gold standard in bedroom Olympics. He lived so long
that his heirs died off one by one. It was his 13th son who
succeeded. So all that reproductive effort came in useful.

Ramesses discovered that if you *don't* win a great battle
you get the historical records to *say* that you did. Or, as a
warrior historian put it …

> 'History will be kind to me for I intend to write it.'
>
> *Winston Churchill (1874–1965), British politician and historian*

The Hittites, in the north of Egypt's empire, were rebelling
and Ramesses II set off to crush them once and for all. He
assembled one of the largest armies Egypt had ever seen –
20,000 men – and marched in the footsteps of Tuthmose III,
200 years earlier.

Ramesses marched on Kadesh and stopped 10 miles
short of the city. Kadesh stood at the fork in a river and a

---

* Or in Alfred's case you burn lots of cakes. Maybe 'Great' was a monkish
misprint and he was really Alfred the Grate?

canal diverted water so it was in effect surrounded by a moat. It would be difficult to attack. Ramesses' hope was to confront the Hittite army and defeat it in open battle. But where was that army? Two Hittite scouts were captured and interrogated. 'The Hittite army is 100 miles to the north,' they claimed.

> 'Appear weak when you are strong, and strong when you are weak.'
>
> *Sun Tzu:* The Art of War

Ramesses ordered his army to march on to Kadesh and set up camp to the west of the city. 'Relax, lads, and take a break,' he must have ordered. But the Great Ramesses had been duped. The captured Hittites were planted there to be caught, interrogated and to lie their socks off.*

The Hittite army was lying to the east of the city, ready to launch a surprise attack on the gullible Ramesses II. The Hittite king, Muwatallis, had an army twice the size of Ramesses' force. Their chariots swept across the plains and caught the Egyptians unprepared. One Egyptian outlying division was scattered as the Hittites sped on towards the main Egyptian camp.

Ramesses found himself isolated with only his shield-bearer, Menna, to help. His elite guard arrived just in time to rescue the pharaoh and to battle the Hittites to a stalemate. Muwatallis withdrew as night fell.

On the second day the Egyptians pulled themselves together and attacked, but the battle was indecisive. Ramesses

---

* The two nameless and forgotten men must have been very courageous to agree to take on such a mission. Once their deception was revealed they would be made to suffer. You have to have a sneaking hope that they escaped.

the Great was a great realist. When Muwatallis proposed a truce, the Egyptian accepted. After all, he must have reasoned, my father Seti couldn't hold Kadesh. A draw is not a bad result.

> 'Never attempt to win by force what can be won by deception.'
>
> *Niccolò Machiavelli:* The Prince

In fact a draw is a very good result if you can march back home and declare that you've won a famous victory. That's what Ramesses did. He had monuments erected and inscriptions carved in temples all over Egypt that portrayed the battle as a triumph.

The images show Ramesses II's mercenaries (in distinctive horned helmets) lopping off the hands of the slain Hittites in order to count the dead. There is a fictional incident of an enemy prince being driven into the River Orontes. He is shown hanging upside down as his subjects try to drain the water from his lungs to revive him – a resuscitation method not to be found in the Bondi Beach lifeguard manual.

After fruitless annual Egypt–Hittite campaigns, both sides finally saw sense and Ramesses II agreed a non-aggression pact. Ramesses said the Hittites sued for peace ... Hittite inscriptions say it was the Egyptians who proposed the truce.

> 'He who wants to persuade should put his trust not in the right argument, but in the right word. The power of sound has always been greater than the power of sense.'
>
> *Joseph Conrad (1857–1924), Polish author:* Lord Jim

Ramesses had mammoth statues built to his glory. The inscriptions told the world how great he was and were deeply chiselled so it would be hard for anyone to wipe him from history. He is remembered in Shelley's poem 'Ozymandias'. Shelley's poetic brain didn't have to work very hard to translate Ramesses II's own tribute to himself ...

> 'King of Kings am I, Ozymandias. If anyone would know how great I am and where I lie, let him surpass one of my works.'
>
> *Inscription on a Ramesses II sculpture*

That was paraphrased by Shelley to read ...

> 'My name is Ozymandias, king of kings:
> Look on my works, ye Mighty, and despair!'

And so Ramesses II made it into the history books as 'the Great'. That's the way to do it.

He was dead by the age of 92. Most people are.

> 'If you live to be one hundred, you've got it made. Very few people die past that age.'
>
> *George Burns (1896–1996), American comedian*

— QUEEN TWOSRET —
(1187–1185 BC), 19th Dynasty

As usual a long reign weakened Egypt and put a spanner in the works of the succession. Mernephta (1213–1203 BC) faced a Libyan invasion in 1207 BC and defeated it. His victory inscription said ...

> 'Libyans slain and their uncircumcised phalluses
> were carried off numbering 6,359.'

Also as usual the Nubians took the opportunity to rebel in the south. They were crushed ... but there is no record of the number of phalluses.

Meneptah's mummy has never been found so some Biblical scholars (with no evidence) leap on that fact and cry, 'Aha! He was probably the pharaoh who pursued the Israelites and was washed away when the Red Sea swamped the Egyptians. Aha!'

The throne passed through short-reigning pharaohs – aged or immature – and to another of those strong women, Queen Twosret, who ruled for her stepson and then for herself (1187–1185 BC).

Twosret's stepson-puppet was Siptah (1193–1187 BC) but he didn't last. His mummy shows he had a club foot. He may have suffered polio myelitis. What's that, you ask? Don't ask me, ask a doctor...

DANGEROUS DAYS DEATH II

POLIO

Polio is caused by an entrovirus. It lives in water contaminated by other people's faeces, so you get infected by drinking a sophisticated cocktail of poo or by not washing your dirty hands after going to the loo. Once inside you, the virus heads for motor neurons in your spine and brain. These are the nerves that control your muscles, and it loves to be there and reproduce.

Very quickly you spike a high fever with a severe headache and stiff neck. All muscles become weak, so swallowing is difficult and it's hard to even pee as your bladder muscles lose strength. Some people recover, although can be left with wasted limbs. If not, then full muscle paralysis gradually occurs over the next few days. When the chest muscles and diaphragm become affected you slowly become shorter and shorter of breath. Then, fully paralysed but conscious, trapped on a bed, with every part of you screaming for breath, motionless, you run out of oxygen and mercifully die.

Dr Peter Fox

Twosret had a strong rival in court – a king-maker called Bay. 'King-maker' was his own opinion. On his tomb an inscription claims …

'I established the king in the seat of his father.'

It was a dangerous game for Bay to play when Queen Twosret was officially the regent. They must have been like two dogs fighting over a bone – the bone comes off worst at first, then the loser of the struggle is next to suffer. So long as Siptah was alive the two could vie to control him. Bay seemed to be the stronger. He used his authority to commission a magnificent tomb for himself. He never got to rest in it.*

When Siptah slipped his mortal coil, Twosret had the bone firmly between her teeth. She declared herself queen

---

* All right. 'Rest' is a bit of a euphemism for a corpse, like 'Not dead but sleeping'. It's a great consolation for the living and the dying. 'He who pretends to look on death without fear, lies.' (Rousseau)

of Egypt as Hatshepsut had 300 years earlier. What would happen to Bay? Historians used to believe he co-ruled with Twosret, but a parchment revealed the cruel truth ...

> 'On this day, it is announced that the pharaoh has killed the great enemy Bay.'

The queen had him executed, of course.

She never enjoyed her power. Bay's supporters rose up in revolt. He'd have been laughing in his tomb ... if he'd been placed in his tomb. Which he wasn't. A civil war split the country and Twosret was the loser. The 19th Dynasty was over. The 20th would flare into life then slowly fade like a torch of tar.

— RAMESSES III —
(1186–1155 BC), 20th Dynasty

> 'A blind bloke walks into a shop with a guide dog. He picks the dog up and starts swinging it around his head. Alarmed, a shop assistant calls out: "Can I help, sir?" "No thanks," says the blind bloke. "Just looking."'
>
> *Tommy Cooper (1921–84), English comedian*

After Ramesses II's reign Egypt began to decline. The world was restless, Troy was besieged and peoples were displaced and roaming the world, looking for a home. Egypt would be as tempting as Eldorado was to the Spanish Conquistadors. It would take a strong pharaoh to lead the resistance.

> 'The foreigners plotted and the people were scattered
> by battle, all at one time. No land could stand before
> their arms.'
>
> *The Harris Papyrus**

No land could withstand the refugee invaders – except
Ramesses III's Egypt, that is. He's been called the 'Last Great
Pharaoh'. The pharaoh ruled effectively enough to defeat an
invasion of 'the Sea People'.†

It was a pincer movement with a land army arriving in the
north-east as a navy headed for the Delta. The land invasion
included women and children in carts, so they were clearly
there to conquer and settle. The Egyptian army met the land
force first and triumphed in a long and bloody battle. A lot of
phalluses were lopped, you have to imagine.

Then Ramesses' forces turned to confront the seaborne
invasion. These were dangerous days to be an invader. The
Egyptians erected palisades of lances stuck in the shore and
hit the landing craft with volleys of arrows. It worked.

> 'As for those who came forward together on the seas,
> the full flame was in front of them at the Nile
> mouths. They were laid low on the beach, slain, and
> made into heaps from head to tail.'
>
> *Egyptian inscription*

---

* This summary of the entire reign of King Ramesses III is a papyrus
41 metres long. It's the longest known papyrus from Egypt – the length
of five London buses. It was found in a tomb across the Nile River from
Luxor, Egypt, and bought by collector Anthony Harris (1790–1869) in
1855; it became part of the British Museum's collection in 1872.

† You might argue that the Sea People would not fight so well in the
deserts of Egypt. Like a fish out of water, you'd think.

Egypt had every reason to be grateful to Ramesses III. They weren't.* The economy was collapsing. Harvests were bad. It seems some natural disaster darkened the skies for two years and caused a famine.

> 'The sun comes but it does not rise. Winter is come in summer, the months come turned backwards and the hours are in disarray.'
>
> *Anonymous: Prayer to Amun (1150 BC)*

Grain prices rose. Ramesses was the focus of the Egyptian people's anger. The tomb builders went on strike four times, demanding their wages be paid in grain – it was inflation-proof.

Yet the greatest threat came from inside his palace. Queen Tiye was leader of a plot to put a new pharaoh on the throne – her son, Pentaweret.

The palace plot

Ramesses III was not expecting this stab in the back – or in the front, as it turned out. The plotters had every chance of success. They made one silly mistake.

Instead of a literal 'stab in the back' their first efforts aimed to get rid of him using magic.

> 'Lost in the mists of antiquity is the origin of the practice of making a small-scale representation of the desired victim, by mutilation or ill treatment of

---

* Winston Churchill led Britain to victory in the Second World War. When the war ended the grateful British people voted him out of power. The great historian Churchill must have expected it.

> which corresponding suffering could be inflicted
> upon the party proposed to be injured.'
>
> C. *L'Estrange Ewen:* Witchcraft and Demonism *(1933)*

We think of effigies as being a feature of the Middle Ages and
the witch-trials of Europe. But the use of effigy magic has
been practised by many cultures for thousands of years.

Did you know ... effigies

Waxed effigies were common in Ancient India, Persia,
Egypt, Africa and Europe. Effigies can be made of clay,
wood and stuffed cloth. They can be marked or painted
to look like the victim, because the closer the effigy
resembles the victim, the more the victim will suffer
when the model is harmed or destroyed.

The theory is pure sympathetic magic. As the effigy
is harmed, so the victim is harmed; when the effigy
is destroyed, so the victim dies.

The Ancient Egyptians often used waxed figures of Apep,
a monster who was the enemy of the sun. The magician
would write Apep's name in green ink on the model, wrap
it in new papyrus and throw it into a fire. As it burned
he kicked it with his left foot four times. The ashes of the
effigy were mixed with excrement and thrown into another
fire.*

If you destroy an image of the king, aiming to harm him,
then in any culture that is 'treason' ... unless it works, of
course, in which case it is a 'coup' – much more acceptable.

---

* I guess that takes real loathing for the victim. The spell books don't say
where you obtain your supply of excrement.

The magic didn't work on Ramesses III – did you really expect it to? More direct action was effective – as we shall see – but the delay was fatal for all concerned.

King killers

> 'It takes two to make a murder. There are born victims, born to have their throats cut, as the cut-throats are born to be hanged.'
>
> *Aldous Huxley (1894–1963), British writer*

Like Julius Caesar hundreds of years later, all Ramesses III's victories didn't make him invulnerable. In 2011 his mummy was examined using modern forensic techniques. All mummies are wrapped in bandages, of course. But there seemed to be rather a lot around Ramesses' neck.

> 'My sore throats are always worse than anyone's.'
>
> *Jane Austen (1775–1817), English novelist*

No, Ms Austen, it is a truth universally acknowledged that Ramesses' sore throat was worse than yours.

Scans of Ramesses III revealed a deep 7cm-wide wound to the throat just under the larynx. Scientists say it was probably caused by a sharp blade and could have led to a rapid death.

The scan also showed a Horus eye charm embedded in the wound – it was probably put there by the Ancient Egyptian embalmers to promote healing. Healing in the afterlife, obviously – they had missed the Ramesses III ambulance in this life.

Regicidal Tiye was taken to court with her fellow palace plotters. It seems Ramesses III died of his wounds before their

case was decided. The trial is recorded in the Great Harris
Papyrus. One of the magicians killed himself before the trial ...

> 'The accused began to make magic scrolls for
> terrifying and to make some models of wax for
> enfeebling the limbs of people. Now when he learned
> of the great crimes of death he had committed, he
> took his own life.'
>
> *Court recorder (1151 BC)*

A wise move for this unnamed accused to kill himself before
suffering at the hands of Ramesses' avengers.

Dozens of people, all of them close to the pharaoh, were
accused of conspiring with Queen Tiye. They included
women from Ramesses III's harem and his butler ... And,
before you say it, yes, the butler did it. The accused also
included a couple of 'inspectors of the harem' – an interesting
role, though we don't have a job description.*

Plotter Oneny had been Captain of the Palace Police.
He was probably the original bent copper. Corruption was
rife. Some of the accused harem women tried to seduce the
judges who were trying their case, but were caught in the
act. Which act? You can guess. Judges who were caught with
their loincloths down were punished harshly.

One of Ramesses III's final acts was to decree ...

> 'May all that they have done fall upon their heads.'

The guilty top plotters were sentenced to death – most
were compelled to commit suicide, maybe by poison, in the

---

* Still, if it were advertised in today's newspapers it might well attract
lengthy queues of applicants at Job Centres around the country.

courtroom itself. (Well, it saves the cost of feeding them in prison, and paying the executioner, while justice is 'seen to be done'.)

Other minor offenders – those who knew of the plot but failed to grass up their friends or family – were sentenced to have ears and noses sliced off. But all those noses and ears didn't save Ramesses III in the end.

In all 38 people were sentenced to death. Tiye's son, Pentaweret, had been lined up to usurp the throne. But was he a weak and parricidal puppet of principal plotter Tiye?

> 'If weakness may excuse,
> What murtherer, what traitor, parricide,
> Incestuous, sacrilegious, but may plead it?
> All wickedness is weakness: that plea therefore
> With God or man will gain thee no remission.'
>
> *John Milton*

What exactly was the fate of Pentaweret?

The scientists who revealed Ramesses' cut throat then turned their attention to the unidentified remains of another body found near Ramesses. DNA tests showed they shared 50 per cent of their DNA, which is typical of a father–son relationship. They had almost certainly found the figurehead of the plot, the king's son Pentaweret.

They found compressed skin folds and wrinkles around this second mummy's neck as well as an inflated chest. That could indicate that the man was strangled to death. The mummy had been known as the Screaming Mummy because it had died with a pained facial expression. Now we know why.

DANGEROUS DAYS DEATH III

STRANGULATION

The sudden tightness and roughness of the cord around your neck comes as a surprise. As you frantically claw at the cord it tightens further, compressing your windpipe and the two carotid arteries either side of the neck. The reflex release of adrenaline, designed to help you fight or flee, causes your heart to race, burning up oxygen faster. Unable to breathe, you can't replace the oxygen, and even if you could no blood is reaching the brain with both carotids blocked.

Starved of its fuel, the brain starts to die. As you become weaker, unable to struggle, the cord tightens further. Eyes popping out and neck veins bulging, you lose consciousness. A few minutes later it's all over: brain dead, heart stopped, expertly strangled to a standstill, you drop to the floor dead. Not that it is much consolation, but at least with a professional it's quick. Amateurs take a bit longer.

Dr Peter Fox

Even in death Ramesses III was abused. His corpse was covered in the skin of a goat – an impure animal in the eyes of the Egyptians (no kidding).

It's a dangerous business, this assassination lark – for killers and killed alike.

One unforeseen consequence of Ramesses' rule was the rise of the Priests of Amun. They took credit for the victory over the Sea People and accumulated the wealth of a pharaoh. It would prove the undoing of the next dynasty.

The palace plotters who killed Ramesses also killed off the glory of Egypt. The land would never be as great again.

— RAMESSES XI —
(1107–1078 BC) 20th Dynasty, and
— HERIHOR —
(1080–1074 BC),
High priest at Thebes during the 20th Dynasty

> 'When I look upon seamen, men of science and philosophers, man is the wisest of all beings; when I look upon priests and prophets nothing is as contemptible as man.'
>
> *Diogenes (412–323 BC), Greek philosopher*

Ramesses III was succeeded by ten more pharaohs all named Ramesses – probably in the hope that the name was great enough to see them through. But Egypt was sliding towards bankruptcy and those powerful priests in Thebes held more wealth than the pharaohs.

By the time of Ramesses XI the priesthood owned two-thirds of all the land in Egypt, 90 per cent of all the ships and much more.

Ramesses XI faced conflict with the priests, whose power was suffocating Egypt. He turned to his enemies for help … he invited the Nubians to overthrow the high priest.

Weak rulers do that. King Vortigern of Britain invited German brothers Hengist and Horsa to help him fight the Pict invaders in the 400s AD and they turned on him. The Nubians would do the same to Ramesses XI and his successors.

The weak and embattled Ramesses XI had needed the support of his army. General Herihor rose to the top of the ranks and, to cover all bases, he also took on the role of High Priest of Amun.* It was natural that the priest-general Herihor should declare himself a rival pharaoh to Ramesses XI.

When Ramesses XI went to that great devourer of souls he took the might of Egypt with him. He left the country bankrupt. The timeless tombs had been robbed. By whom? By Ramesses XI.

Herihor and the priests set up an alternative kingdom in Thebes, the Lower Kingdom. The 21st Dynasty set up in the Nile Delta – the Upper Kingdom. So the crowns of Upper and Lower were divided again.

The country was to be reunited in 943 BC under the 22nd Dynasty. But it was a patched vase, glued together and too weak to stay in one piece for long.

---

* If Herihor had been in Italy a couple of thousand years later, he'd have been a mix of the Pope and Mussolini.

FADING PHARAOHS

DYNASTIES 21 TO 26
THE THIRD
INTERMEDIATE PERIOD
(1069–525 BC)

'Behind me the branches of a wasted and sterile existence are cracking.'

Gustav Mahler (1860–1911), German composer

The cracks were beginning to deepen and the old order to crumble. Pharaohs were no longer revered as gods. Mere mortals were walking in the sandals of the pharaoh-gods but walking with all the needs and greeds and cruelties and cunning of fallible humans. The great pharaohs were gone and the spectres of famine and bankruptcy, invaders and civil war were haunting the world of the Nile.

'To keep any great nation up to a high standard of civilisation there must be enough superior characters to hold the balance of power, but the very moment the balance of power gets into the hands of second-rate men and women, a decline of that nation is inevitable.'

Christian D. Larson (1874–1954),
American New Thought leader and teacher

The second-rate leaders were on the march. The downhill march.

'It's easier to go down a hill than up it but the view is much better at the top'

Henry Ward Beecher (1813–87),
*American Congregationalist clergyman**

In the Third Intermediate Period weak dynasties came and disappeared. Some pharaohs, like Sheshonq (945–924 BC, 22nd Dynasty), flexed their muscles in an imitation of the pharaohs of days long gone. Sheshonq invaded Palestine. Was this a sign of Egypt on the road to recovery? Not really. The aggressive Pharaoh Sheshonq was actually a Libyan invader who had seized the throne.

---

* An expert in going downhill. This pillar of the church was famed for his serial adultery and the sensational trials that ensued. He died in his sleep after a stroke. Naturally.

— SHESHONQ I —
(943–922 BC), 22nd Dynasty

> 'Far better is it to dare mighty things, to win glorious
> triumphs, even though checkered by failure ... than
> to rank with those poor spirits who neither enjoy nor
> suffer much, because they live in a grey twilight that
> knows not victory nor defeat.'
>
> *Theodore Roosevelt*

Twilight usually lasts half an hour. In Egypt the so-called twilight lasted a thousand years from the divided land at the end of Ramesses XI's 20th Dynasty reign to the arrival of the Romans. One very long and slow decline.

Those pharaoh-priests at Thebes fought among themselves as much as with invaders or their north-Egypt cousins. The dynasty that finally gave Egypt a sort of unity was the 22nd, led by Sheshonq I from Libya.

In the end it was easy enough. Sheshonq ruled in the north then appointed his sons as governors and arch-priests in Thebes to the south. He then went on to make the country rich and stable by conquering neighbours in the Middle East. He arrived at Jerusalem and was bought off.

> 'He was given the treasures of the house of the Lord,
> and the treasures of the king's house and he took
> away all the shields of gold King Solomon had made.'
>
> *I Kings 14*

It made sense. Golden shields are useless in battle and Solomon was dead so he wouldn't mind.

That doesn't sound like a civilisation in decline. But not every pharaoh was to prove as strong as Sheshonq.

— OSORKON III —
(787–759 BC), 22nd Dynasty

'When you have to kill a man, it costs nothing to be polite.'

Winston Churchill

When it came to killing men, Osorkon was anything but polite. He took over the priesthood of Amun in Thebes and he encountered some opposition. He could have negotiated or banished the rebels, but Osorkon went further. Having captured the rebel leaders he went to the temple and made offerings ... that was so the gods would approve his ruthless revenge, and so his subjects could see it didn't pay to mess with Osorkon.

Then he had the bodies of the executed men burned. That put paid to their happy ending in the next life. It was vindictive and provocative.

His opponents weren't cowed for long. They simmered and planned their own revenge under a new leader, Pedubast. He declared himself king and the first of a new dynasty, the 23rd. Naturally this was a red rag to the Osorkon bully. It meant civil war ... again. Another crack in the megalith of Egypt.

All because a prince burned the corpses of his enemies, and his enemies believed it mattered because of the ancient superstition that bodies were needed in the afterlife.

When the Old Kingdom pharaohs were preserved in bandages it was a harmless eccentricity. But now *everyone* was claiming the right to mummification. The Egyptians were not fools, so their attitude must have been, 'Hey! Maybe you DON'T need a body in the next life ... but why take the risk?'

> 'Ah, yes, superstition: it would appear to be cowardice in face of the supernatural.'
>
> *Theophrastus*

Superstition. Rival pharaohs went to ruinous war over a batch of burned bodies. Superstition was tearing the ancient kingdom apart.

— PIYE —
(747–716), 25th Dynasty

> 'I am monarch of all I survey,
> My right there is none to dispute,
> From the centre all round to the sea,
> I am lord of the fowl and the brute.'*
>
> *William Cowper (1731–1800)*

While the Egyptians squabbled, their old subjects in Nubia were quietly shaking loose their Egyptian pharaoh fetters and re-establishing the old kingdom of Kush. In 747 BC the throne of Kush passed to King Piye. He bided his time then, in 728 BC, he struck.

---

* Though to be fair, the 'monarch' of Cowper's poem was Alexander Selkirk, a.k.a. Robinson Crusoe. Being monarch of a desert island was his hollow boast made with bitterness. Piye at least had something to survey – a rich and ancient kingdom.

Like so many warriors before and since he would claim,
'Well, *they* started it.' Pharaoh Tefnakht (727–720 BC, of the
short-lived 24th Dynasty) united the squabbling, brawling,
regal rivals of the north to march south and attack Piye's
allies. Piye rose to defend his friends, marched north … and
kept going. He took Middle Egypt and then Lower Egypt
and could claim to be monarch of all he surveyed.

The kingdom was in the hands of a foreign ruler again. Yet
Piye was more Egyptian than many of his predecessors. He
was a passionate fan of the god Amun. His soldiers had to
cleanse themselves before going into battle, while he himself
made sacrifices to the chief god. The Egyptians must have
felt as if they had been attacked by the local vicar with a band
of well-armed monks.

It wasn't only force that prevailed. Piye had creative
thinking on his side too. When he reached Memphis the
city closed its gates and resisted. Piye wasn't a medieval
warlord with siege engines in his weaponry. Instead he used
his imagination. The city was closed, but the harbour, full of
sailing vessels, was open.

The practical Piye used the masts and rigging from the
ships to construct scaling ladders. His cleansed cohorts
climbed the walls.

> 'To invent, you need a good imagination and a pile
> of junk.'
>
> *Thomas A. Edison (1847–1931), Inventor of the phonograph,
> the motion picture camera and the electric light bulb*

The battle was bloody but conclusive. Piye prevailed.

The four pharaohs who had divided Egypt surrendered to
Piye, who then went home to Nubia and never set foot in
Egypt again.

Having established the 25th Dynasty, he then died. He was buried in a pyramid in Nubia and probably went serenely on to join Amun the sun god.

Piye in the sky.

Mouse power

The world was moving on and the glories of Egypt's past counted for little. The Assyrians became the new conquistadors of the Middle East. They eyed Egypt but Piye's successor, Pharaoh Shabaka (716–702 BC) kept King Sargon II of Assyria at bay for a while.

The Assyrians invaded in 667 BC and sacked the southern capital, Thebes, three years later.

Tanutamani (died 653 BC), the last of the Nubian kings to succeed Piye, fled south back to his old Nubian home. In the north the Assyrians had purged the nobility as thoroughly as Robespierre would do in the French Revolution – all bar one were executed. You can understand why Tanutamani discretely withdrew. Those Assyrians didn't mess about.

The Assyrians left a client king, a satrap, in charge, but focused their control in the north. Into the vacuum in Thebes, to the south, stepped a new dynasty.

The Assyrians were back under a new king, Sennacherib (705–681 BC). He was just as dangerous to the Egyptians as Sargon. Even the appearance of Sennacherib's Assyrian troops made enemies faint away with fear. He boasted …

'They had seen the approach of my cavalry and they had heard the roar of the mighty troops and their hearts became afraid. The city I captured, I carried off its spoil, I destroyed, I devastated, and I burned with fire.'

Monument inscription

No wonder the Egyptians refused to fight. However there is a legendary tale of Sennacherib's ultimate defeat at the hands of Pharaoh Sethos. According to the ever-unreliable Herodotus …

'Sennacherib, king of the Arabians and Assyrians, marched his vast army into Egypt, the warriors one and all refused to come to the aid of Pharaoh Sethos. The monarch, greatly distressed, entered into the temple and, before the image of the god, bewailed the fate which impended over him.

As he wept he fell asleep, and dreamed that the god came and stood at his side, telling him be of good cheer, and go boldly forth to meet the Assyrian host, which would do him no hurt. The god himself would send those who should help him.

Sethos collected such of the Egyptians as were willing to follow him, who were none of them warriors, but traders, artisans, and market people; and with these marched to Pelusium, which commands the entrance into Egypt, and there pitched his camp.

As the two armies lay here opposite one another, there came in the night a multitude of field-mice, which devoured all the quivers and bowstrings of the enemy, and ate the thongs by which the Assyrians managed their shields. Next morning they began their fight, and great multitudes fell, as they had no arms with which to defend themselves.*

There stands to this day in the temple of Vulcan, a stone statue of Sethos, with a mouse in his hand, and an inscription to this effect – "Look on me, and learn to reverence the gods."'

---

* Herodotus doesn't mention what the mice did to the Assyrian swords. Sword-swallowing mice?

Trounced by tradesmen, gutted by grocers and massacred by mice. What an Assyrian disgrace. In 627 BC two of Sennacherib's treacherous sons loosened the statue of an Assyrian god from its mounting so it was ready to topple. The monstrous idol had a lion's body, eagle's wings, and human head. The patricidal pair lured Sennacherib beneath the statue then tipped it onto him.

So Sethos had seen off one Assyrian warlord. But his success went to the heads of his successors. 'Let's take on the Assyrians,' they roared, and sided with the Palestinians against Assyria. Sadly the vigour of the young dynasty was just a mirage in the Sahara.

> 'Your old men shall dream dreams, your young men shall see visions.'
>
> *Joel 2:28*

Sennacherib's son Esarhaddon (681–669 BC) had succeeded to the Assyrian throne. (He was not one of the father-flattening sons.) He led an invasion that was driving Egyptian armies south and into oblivion.

In the Assyrian way he didn't wait to be told how great he was. Esarhaddon announced to the world ...

> 'I am powerful, I am all-powerful, I am a hero, I am gigantic, I am colossal ... I am without an equal among all kings.'
>
> *Assyrian Chronicle*

You wouldn't want to step on his toes then. But you could have whispered in his ear a little warning ...

> 'Vain-glorious men are the scorn of the wise, the admiration of fools, the idols of paradise, and the slaves of their own vaunts.'
>
> *Sir Francis Bacon (1561–1626),*
> *English statesman, scientist and author*

The chronicle of his reign goes on to explain that, in the 12th year of his reign, Esarhaddon of Assyria went to Egypt. He fell sick on the road, and died.

Letting your leader die is a tactical mistake for any invader. Egypt's old friend, Death, had stepped in to save it. Egypt exulted. The rodents rejoiced – probably. (This time the mice were not required to start nobbling the enemy with nibbling.)

But it was only a respite. A breather. A half-time slice of orange.

The vision of defeating Assyria failed to allow for the reality that the Assyrian enemy was now ruled by Esarhaddon's son – the merciless Ashurbanipal (668–627 BC). He was not a man of straw, a scarecrow, a dummy, a mannequin. He was a miffed man, an angry Assyrian. In 633 BC he invaded Egypt to finish off what his dead dad had started.

Many of the Egyptian nobility were executed and the Assyrians ruled for 20 painful years. Ashurbanipal was a cruel ruler:

> 'I had the arms and legs cut off their bodies and I fed them to the dogs, pigs, wolves and eagles. I fed them to the birds in the heavens and the fish in the oceans. What was left I had taken from Babylon and thrown into heaps.
>
> I broke into the tombs of the old Elamite kings and let in the sun. I carried their bones back to Assyria. I

> stopped the priests giving them sacrifices so their
> ghosts were tormented.'
>
> *Ashurbanipal monument*

Nice man.

The Assyrian Empire took over in the north and their satraps ruled. But even the mighty Assyria began to fail. Rival empires hovered like vultures. When the Assyrian homeland was threatened, Egyptians fought for Assyria's enemies. In 612 BC a joint force of Scythians and Persians attacked the capital Nineveh and extinguished the royal Assyrian line.

Assyria had fallen. No cause for celebrations along the Nile. Egypt was next on the Persian hit-list.

DYNASTIES 27 TO 31
THE LATE PERIOD
(525–332 BC)

> 'Humankind cannot bear very much reality.'
>
> *T.S. Eliot:* Four Quartets

In 539 BC powerful Persians conquered Babylon then went on to take over Egypt. Persians had become the ancient world's top dogs. They paid Egypt the greatest insult of all. They didn't kick the feeble Egyptian people while they were down. They ignored them. They were absentee landlords who left the ruling in the hands of their civil servant satraps.

Eventually the Egyptians summoned up the strength to rebel in 405 BC. The resurgent natives held on till 343 BC, then the Persians rallied. Egyptian Pharaoh Nectanebo II did what any wise ruler would and he ran away. No one knew, no one could have guessed, that he would be the last native Egyptian to rule Egypt.* (Maybe. More of that later.)

Piye may have brought a sort of unity to the shambles of the Third Intermediate Period. But the Saharan sands were trickling through the hourglass of history. Invaders were driven out by another wave of invaders. Mayfly pharaohs came and disappeared – important to themselves, but little noticed in the widening world of Persia and Greece and Rome.

> 'Land and sea, weakness and decline are great
> separators, but death is the great divorcer for ever.'
>
> *John Keats (1795–1821), English romantic poet*

Empires are like animals. They grow and grow till they are consuming all around. Then they become obese and old and start to decline. Younger animals – the very ones they bullied when they were in their pomp – start to tear them down. All that is left are the bones. It happens to them all. Some last a hundred years. Egypt two thousand. The Third Reich a dozen.†

> 'The woods decay, the woods decay and fall,
> Man comes and tills the field and lies beneath,
> And after many a summer dies the swan.'
>
> *Alfred Lord Tennyson (1809–92), British Poet Laureate, in 'Tithonus'*

---

* Until the modern era, that is. A 2,300-year dearth of native rule. When empires burn they take an eternity to rise from the ashes.

† Of course Mr Hitler said, 'I intend to set up a thousand-year Reich.' But Hitler (in the words of Winston Churchill) was a 'bloodthirsty guttersnipe'. He was also as deluded as the pharaohs in their quest for immortality.

BRIEF TIMELINE

DECLINE OF THE PHARAOHS

945 BC   The Libyans are coming from the west. They will
           overthrow the priests of Amun who have ruled
           from Thebes. Twenty pharaohs in 200 years is
           weak and unstable.

747 BC   Now it's the turn of the Nubians under Piye to
           move north and conquer Egypt.

669 BC   Assyrians conquer and rule Egypt.

525 BC   Invasion of the Persians.

343 BC   And the Persians are back.

332 BC   Alexander the Great arrives, the Macedonians
           rule. They found Alexandria. A Macedonian
           dynasty will rule until 31 BC.

51 BC   Cleopatra on the throne.

30 BC   Egypt is part of the Roman Empire.

AD 642   Arab conquest of Egypt. Egypt becomes Islamic.
           The ancient gods are dead.

⟶ AHMOSE II ⟵
(570–526 BC), 26th Dynasty

> 'Anger is as a stone cast into a wasp's nest.'
>
> *Pope Paul VI (1897–1978)*

If your neighbours are as dangerous as a wasp's nest then you don't go throwing stones. Pharaoh Apries (589–570 BC) felt threatened by the expanding Greek state in the Mediterranean. So he attacked it in 570 BC. Bad idea.

The Egyptians were thrashed and the native Egyptian soldiers in a rebellious mood. Apart from a needless war they saw foreign mercenaries being treated better than loyal Egyptians. In stepped the popular General Ahmose to lead a rebellion and take the pharaoh's crown.*

Even this astute leader didn't have a crystal ball to see where the next threat was coming from. He befriended the Greeks across the Mediterranean Sea. He failed to see the growing power to the north-east. King Cyrus the Great united the Medes and the Persians in 550 BC and began rolling up countries on the long and dusty road to Egypt's borders.

By 530 BC Cyrus was on Ahmose's doorstep and waiting for a sign of weakness. It came the moment Ahmose died. Persia invaded; Ahmose's son, Psatmik III, was left to face the mighty Persian Empire.

He lost. He fled.

---

* Awful Apries fled to the court of his enemy, the king of Babylon. He returned with an army three years later to reclaim his throne. He was beaten and died – either in the battle or executed by the Egyptian victors. Some people just can't let sleeping wasps lie.

∼ CAMBYSES II ∼
(525–522 BC), 27th Dynasty, and
THE PERSIANS

> 'Rejoice, O ye nations, with his people: for he will
> avenge the blood of his servants, and will render
> vengeance to his adversaries.'
>
> *Deuteronomy 32:43*

The Persians arrived, led by Cambyses. Why did he feel
the need to annexe Egypt when Persia already had such a
thriving empire to manage? Herodotus (writing just 70 years
after the invasion) gave three reasons:

🐫 Legend has it this warrior invaded because the
Egyptians had upset his mother – mummy's boy turned
mummies' boy, you could say. He said he would 'turn
Egypt upside down' and was as good as his word.

🐫 Another story said he requested an Egyptian princess
as a wife and was furious when he was fobbed off
with a woman of lower rank. (The woman in question
probably wasn't overjoyed herself.)

🐫 Cambyses claimed to be the illegitimate son of the
daughter of Pharaoh Apries. He was therefore the
rightful heir to Cyrus's throne – usurped by the dead
Ahmose.

Herodotus says all three stories are suspect. They were
Persian propaganda created to justify the invasion. But
invade they did, with the help of a traitor.

Cambyses and his Persian forces crossed the desert.
They were met by an Egyptian general named Phanes who

defected to them and passed on military secrets. When the Egyptians finally confronted Phanes, and his new-found Persian friends, they came up with a grim revenge.

They marched Phanes' sons into the no-man's land between the two armies where their father could see them. The Egyptians then slit the throats of the boys over a large bowl. Wine and water were added to the bowl and the Egyptian troops drank it as the Persians looked on.

This terror tactic did them no good. The Egyptians were routed and the Persian depredations were grim. The invaders ripped a mummified body from its tomb and burned it; Cambyses himself stabbed the sacred bull of Memphis.*

Cambyses also killed his half-brother Bardiya to secure the throne. He kept the murder a secret and conspired with a priest who declared he *was* the living Bardiya. It was a b-i-g mistake on Cambyses' part. While Cambyses was absent in Egypt, the phoney Bardiya started taking over his empire – he suspended taxes for three years so, naturally, the people of Persia supported him. (Wouldn't you?)

Cambyses marched from Egypt to meet the Bardiya impostor but died on the way. The fake Bardiya took over but only lasted seven months. In typical fashion for those dangerous days, he was assassinated. Darius (550–486 BC) – one of the seven knife-wielding assassins – took over the Persian Empire and became Egypt's new ruthless ruler.

Darius ruled Egypt as another absentee landlord – it was small fry in his empire. Darius was as pitiless as Cambyses. Take the warrior, Aryander, who was left to rule Egypt and decided to cash in. He had coins with Darius's head on and melted them down because the gold content was worth more

---

* Don't worry, it was given a ceremonial burial with all the honours of a pharaoh. It didn't end up as medium-rare steak served up with potatoes on a Persian platter.

than the coins. But melting his king's head was 'treason' and Darius had him executed. Heads you lose.

— NECTANEBO II —
(360–343 BC), 30th Dynasty

'It is easier for a father to have children than for children to have a real father.'

Pope John XXIII (1881–1963)

'It is a wise father that knows his own child.'

William Shakespeare

The Egyptians rebelled against cruel Persian rule. Egyptian pharaohs ruled one last time until Nectanebo II was defeated and the Persian returned. Nectanebo was then the last native Egyptian to wear the crowns of Egypt … or was he?

The Persians and the Egyptians had battled for Egypt using Greek mercenaries. It was only a matter of time before the Greeks took the country for themselves. The all-conquering Alexander the Great was the man for the job and he would implant Greek bloodlines into the pharaohs' palaces.

If you believe the history books, Nectanebo was the last pharaoh of Egyptian blood. But if we believe the legends, then he wasn't. The last native Egyptian was someone far more remarkable.

Nectanebo simply vanished. His grave hasn't been discovered. His sarcophagus *has* been found and rests in the British Museum. It was never used as a coffin, though it had been converted into a bath in Egyptian times.

The enemy of Persia was Macedonia – northern Greece. The story goes that Nectanebo fled to Macedonia when the Persians overran his country again. The King of Macedonia was Philip II and the former pharaoh was welcomed to his court where he was feted as a great Egyptian magician. According to the scandal-mongers, Philip's wife Olympias welcomed Nectanebo to her bed.*

The result of their liaison was baby Alexander, who went on to rule the world as Alexander the Great – son of Nectanebo.

So the last pharaoh of Egyptian blood was…? Yes. Alexander the Great.

That is such an unlikely story isn't it? But there is another legend …

The assassination of Philip II

Philip was going to the theatre. He wanted to impress his Greek guests by walking through the streets to demonstrate just what a man of the people he was. The attack, when it came, was by his own bodyguard, Pausanias of Orestis. The assassin tried to escape and reach his friends, who were waiting for him with horses.† He was chased by three of Philip's bodyguards, but tripped on a vine-root and was

---

* Olympias wasn't her real name. Hubby Philip's horse won the Olympic Games so he renamed her in its honour. (After a win on the Grand National you may wish to rename your wife Red Rum.) Her birth name was rather more prosaic: Myrtle. Alexander must have been pleased about her name change when he grew up to conquer the world. It just sounds all wrong – Alexander the Great, Lord of the world, son of Myrtle.

† So, Monsieur Poirot, your grey cells will deduce from that that the murder was premeditated?

speared by his pursuers. He was of course unable to explain what lay behind the assassination.*

Alexander had Pausanias's corpse crucified — he was cross – but Olympias built a memorial to her husband's assassin.

Historians have never satisfactorily explained what lay behind the killing. A Roman historian said assassin Pausanias was the lover of Philip II and they'd had a tiff.

The people suspected of facilitating Pausanias's assassination attempt include young Alexander and his mother Olympias. It seems the widow-queen placed a crown on the coffin of the assassin. Alexander the heir had all the world to gain.†

Historians say Alexander's involvement is nonsense. (And you may hesitate before plotting the murder of your own dear dad.) BUT … what if Olympias and Alex knew Philip II WASN'T Alexander's father? Then Philip was just some bloke who stood in the way of Alexander and world domination?

Makes you think.

But the story of the Greeks in Egypt is another story for another chapter.

---

* In much the same way as Lee Harvey Oswald, the assassin of President Kennedy in 1963, was killed before he could explain his motives. Gossip abhors a vacuum, so conspiracy theories rush to fill it. Oswald was the tool of the Russians, the CIA, the Texas branch of the Women's Institute or alien invaders … or all of them.

† Olympias was helping her son to power but needed a little more in the way of motivation. This charming lady was said to have slaughtered the daughter of King Philip II and his sixth wife, Cleopatra, before driving Cleopatra herself to suicide.

TERROR OF
THE TOMBS

> 'Nesamun took us up and showed us the tomb of King
> Ramesses VI ... And I spent four days breaking into
> it, we being present all five. We opened the tomb and
> entered it. We found a cauldron of bronze and three
> wash bowls of bronze.'
>
> *Record of grave-robber's trial*

The pyramids were huge billboards advertising the
affluence of the aristocracy. A sign that said to the good
citizens, 'Look how great we are.' To the scoundrels it said,
'Free meals for life ... if you can get in.'

After a couple of thousand years the robbers had
overcome every obstacle created to confound the cunning
kleptomaniacs. By 1500 BC the priests moved the royal
tombs hundreds of miles south to the Valley of the Kings.
The coffins and treasures were buried in caves tunnelled into
the rock.

The tombs in the Valley of the Kings range in size from graves that are little more than a hole in the ground to extensive tombs with over a hundred underground chambers. Many passageways and shafts were there to confound the robbers. They didn't work.

Each tomb had only one way in and that was blocked with stone to keep out the thieves. Yet still the tombs were trashed.

― PROFILE OF PANEB ―

'There's a difference between criminals and crooks. Crooks steal. Criminals blow some guy's brains out. I'm a crook.'

Ronald Biggs (1929–2013), English thief and Great Train Robber

What makes one person a paragon and another a parasitic pest? One of the names that has trickled through time is Paneb – serial scoundrel.

Around 1200 BC he was one of a family of tomb-workers in the Valley of the Kings near Thebes. These families worked hard and lived modest lives while surrounded by fortunes they couldn't earn in a thousand lifetimes. Paneb married and had nine children. He also had three married girlfriends to support.

Apart from his marital infidelities he was a shifty individual. When the post of foreman came up it should have passed to the dead foreman's younger brother. (It was nepotism, but an accepted part of Egyptian culture.) Paneb filched the foreman's job by that other common cultural practice – bribery. He bribed the vizier.

That was against the law. To cover his tracks, Paneb committed the ultimate act of audacity and made a complaint against the vizier so that his benefactor was sacked.

> 'Freeze, freeze, thou bitter sky,
> That dost not bite so nigh, as benefits forgot.'
>
> *William Shakespeare*: As You Like It

Now he was in the driving seat. He had a large workforce at his disposal, a force that he could direct to profitable projects of his own – digging a fine tomb for himself was a predictable way to abuse his power.

Then Pharaoh Seti II died in 1192 BC and the key to riches was in Paneb's sweaty hands … as were precious incense, wine and a statue from the king's tomb. Stone pillars and doors for the king's tomb were diverted to Paneb's own gravesite.

You can sense he was beginning to over-reach himself. His easy success went to his head.

> 'What comes over a man, is it soul or mind
> That to no limits and bounds he can stay confined?
> That though there is no fixed line between wrong
>   and right,
> There are roughly zones whose laws must be obeyed?'
>
> *Robert Frost (1874–1963), US poet: 'There Are Roughly Zones'*

In a drunken stupor he beat up nine men in one night and threatened to kill his own father. But he really crossed the line of acceptable behaviour when he was seen to insult the pharaohs in the worst possible way – he sat on the sarcophagus of Seti II. One might almost say he used Seti as a settee.

His next big mistake was to make an enemy of a man called Amenakht who reported all of Paneb's crimes. For good measure, Amenakht threw in an accusation that Paneb had murdered two of the pharaoh's messengers.*

These accusations were unproven. But more charges followed. In one a workman said Paneb stole a bed ... and the workman was lying on it at the time.

The real clincher was the charge that he had stolen a model goose from the grave of Pharaoh Ramesses II's wife. Paneb swore his innocence. The authorities searched his house and found the goose. You can imagine the constable's glee, can't you?

'Got you bang to rights there, Paneb me old son.'

'Goose? How did that get there? Never seen it in me life, guv.'

Paneb was found guilty on that charge.

We don't know his fate after that. He died aged around 67 (and was buried in a smart, expertly-crafted tomb). Did he die of old age? Or something more violent? Because stealing from a royal tomb was frowned on. Scowled upon.

There is an ambiguous clue to his fate. A document dating from the reign of Ramesses III refers to the 'killing of the chief'. This chief could well have been Paneb, but there is no name mentioned. If the law took its usual course then he would have faced capital punishment.

---

* Amenakht's complaints are recorded in a papyrus that was bought by Egyptologist Henry Salt, so it's known as the Salt Papyrus. Just as well it wasn't bought by Henry Pepper.

— RISK OF ROBBERY —

'Punishment is not for revenge, but to lessen crime
and reform the criminal.'

Elizabeth Fry (1780–1845), English prison reformer

The penalty for being caught robbing a grave was torture, then execution. The rewards for getting away with it obviously outweighed the horror of being impaled on a stake.

To lessen the risk, it made sense to invest a bit of money before you set out. First priority would be to make sure the local officials were on your side. Then recruit a team – you couldn't expect to do this alone. It seems a gang of seven or eight was the optimum; any more and you'd get in one another's way … and have to divide the loot too many times.

The grave gang would be made up of people with special skills. You'd need …

- Expert stonemasons to chisel their way in would be the obvious choice.

- A smith on hand to melt down your gold and silver in case the palace police came knocking at your door.

- A ferryman. The Valley of the Kings is on the west bank of the Nile – the sunset side – from Thebes. So a boatman (or getaway driver) to get you across (and back with the booty) was handy – he could also be your lookout.

- General labourers to carry away the debris and act as water-carriers for the masons.

The valley is composed of different rock formations – some softer than others. Ideally, you'd have found a way through the softer rock to make your own back door. That way it would take longer for the priests to discover the loss, giving you time to make your getaway. If you had to go through the front door, you'd need to make sure the seal looked intact.

— THE GRAVE-ROBBER'S GUIDE —

> 'Honesty is for the most part less profitable than dishonesty.'
>
> *Plato (428–348 BC), Greek philosopher*

A dozen trial reports have survived. They give a useful hint on how to rob a pharaoh's tomb. A stonemason called Amun-pnufer made a confession in 1110 BC giving details of how he'd helped rob tombs from the 17th Dynasty. He explained how he'd set fire to coffins so the gold decoration would melt into puddles and be easier to remove.

Of course the easiest way to win the treasures of the tombs – provided you could afford to make an investment up front – was to bribe everyone concerned with the burial. These would include perhaps …

◘ The coffin-maker. He can manufacture one end of the coffin to be a trapdoor, saving you the bother of breaking the seals and forcing up the heavy lid to get at the mummy. You'd just slide the body out of the end.

◘ The tomb-sealer. He must be seen to seal each set of doors. Pay him enough and he would make sure the two interior doors were not sealed. A lot less work for you later on.

- ◪ The tomb guards. Security guards lead a boring life. (Some things never change.) Pay them to turn a blind eye or two. They might welcome the spice of a grave-robbery. As a robber, you'd tidy up after you and make sure you left the grave apparently undisturbed. Those guards could go on pretending to guard the tomb long after you'd emptied it.

- ◪ The priests. The problem is they are men of substance. You probably can't afford to pay them up front. They will be more susceptible to bribery if you offer them a share of the booty – after all, they know what is in there and may have their eyes on a prize or two.

Once you are inside there are some odd tricks of the trade you can use. For example, you could start a fire inside the tomb. The gold will melt and puddle and save you scraping the gold leaf off the furniture.

One Ancient Egyptian tip is equally relevant to today's bank-robbers: don't spend too much of your swag at once. Many naive tomb-robbers gave themselves away by splashing out too much loot too soon and arousing suspicion.

The most successful tomb-robbers were the architects – they knew the passages and traps well because they had designed them. Gamekeepers turned poachers.

— THE KUSHY LIFE —

'A great empire, like a great cake, is most easily diminished at the edges.'

Benjamin Franklin (1706–90), American statesman

Egypt is famous for its pyramids. Yet there were far more pyramids built by its southern neighbours in Kush.

Around 1500 BC, the pharaohs sent armies in to overpower Kush. For nearly 500 years, Kush would be ruled by the Egyptians, and pay the Egyptian taxes, of course – the universal punishment for losing a war.

Then, around 1000 BC, the people of Kush were able to turn the tables, and win their independence. By 724 BC they went a step further and, led by the Kushite King Piye, a powerful Kushite army was able to invade Egypt and control it. Kushite kings ruled there for a couple of hundred years and the kingdom along the Nile was a mighty 1,500 miles long.

In 671 BC, the Assyrians, with better weapons, were able to drive the Kushites out of Egypt, and rule it for themselves. Yet that was far from being a disaster for the Kingdom of Kush. The Kush people withdrew to their original borders and the Kingdom of Kush entered a golden age. Even when the Assyrian pharaoh invaded Kush and destroyed its capital city Napata, the Kush built a better new capital at Meroe … 300 miles to the south and out of reach of their nasty neighbours.

For the next 150 years, the Kushites grew wealthy. They were able to build fine cities. Another name for Kush was Nubia and the word 'nub' is Egyptian for gold. The Kush were sitting on a goldmine – literally.

Even when the Romans, at the height of their power, arrived in Kush in 27 BC the Kushites were able to resist. Roman Emperor Augustus demanded that the Kush pay him tax. The Kush, under warrior queen Amanirenas, replied by attacking the Roman encampments in Egypt and forcing the invaders to make peace. This tough lady was described by historian Strabo as 'a very masculine sort of woman, and blind in one eye'. She lost it fighting against the Romans. Well if you're going to go around picking fights with Romans you have to expect to lose a few body bits.*

> 'Ambassadors from Kush obtained everything for which they asked. And the Roman Emperor even remitted the taxes that he had levied on the region.'
> · *Strabo (64 BC—AD 24), Greek historian*

The Roman lesson was learned – as Augustus never said, 'It doesn't pay to brush with the Kush, mush.'

To add insult to injury, the Kushite army took a statue of Augustus and knocked its head off. The head was buried under the door frame of an important building so everyone who entered walked over the Emperor of Rome. The ultimate slight.

So Kush thrived in its independence. It became known for its wealth. And, as is the way of history, such ostentatious affluence attracts jealous neighbours. The good days were ended by a people known as the Axums, who invaded from the East around AD 500.

> 'Jealousy is a dog's bark which attracts thieves.'
> *Karl Kraus (1874–1936), Austrian writer and satirist*

---

* Please, no smart-alec remarks about how Amanirenas never saw eye-to-eye with Emperor Augustus.

The Kush customs (or Kushtoms, if you prefer)

> 'Elaborate burial customs are a sure sign of decadence.'
>
> *J.G. Ballard (1930–2009), English novelist*

Naturally much of the Egyptian way of life rubbed off on the Kingdom of Kush – with a difference or two. Their pyramids, for example, were usually flat-topped.

They adopted many Egyptian gods, though their original top god was a lion with a difference – he had three heads.

As well as pyramids the Kush kings were often buried in mass graves, along with courtiers and animals. They would dig a pit and put stones around them in a circle.

King Piye defeated Egypt and founded the 25th Dynasty, ruling 752–721 BC. But his heart belonged to Kush. He was taken home to be buried. Egyptian pharaohs had been buried in the Valley of the Kings. But Piye wanted a pyramid like the ancient pharaohs, so naturally he got one. It was the first pyramid to be built for 500 years.

His four favourite horses were buried with him. Of course they had to be killed first, which seems a bit tough on the creatures.*

> 'Does not the gratitude of the dog put to shame any man who is ungrateful to his benefactors?'
>
> *Saint Basil (AD 330–379), Greek bishop*

---

* That rather scuppers the theory about horseshoes being lucky. Those four nags had 16 between them and didn't have a lot of luck.

Yet Piye was renowned for his love of horses. An inscription tells of him marching into a defeated city where he discovered the horses had been mistreated. He said ...

> 'I swear by the gods that love me, I swear by the fresh air in my nose that your greatest crime was not to fight me. It was to beat and starve your horses.'

Still, he was not as brutal as the old Kush kings who preferred human sacrifices. You have to be dead first, so it's pretty safe to omit the warning, 'Don't try this at home.'

◄ Have your funeral director take six of your favourite wives and six prisoners of war.

◄ Have them marched off to your pyramid and led to the room where you are lying peacefully in your sarcophagus.

◄ Have your guards whack them on the head with a heavy instrument till they are as dead as you.

◄ Lay the corpses in neat rows beside you. Then seal the pyramid.

As well as these bed-mates and servants in your afterlife, you'll probably need your hounds to go hunting, so have them killed too. Even camels were buried in the Kush pyramids.

Piye's four horses were a conservative number to pull his chariot through the afterlife. In a pyramid near Kurru there were twenty-four horses buried with the Kush king.

There is a contradiction in the Kush religion. They believed that the spirit (or Ka) of the deceased has wings. It can fly through the afterlife. So why does it need a horse-drawn chariot?

Relatively dead

> 'My grandmother was a very tough woman. She buried three husbands ... and two of them were just napping.'
>
> *Rita Rudner (1953—) American comedian, actress*

The prisoners of war were there to slave for the dead pharaoh. But not all the sacrificial victims were slaves. Modern DNA testing has revealed that in several Kush burial mounds and pyramids the corpses were related to the dead pharaoh. He had his relatives killed to accompany him into the afterlife.

There are no signs of violence on these skeletons so if they all died to keep the pharaoh company they must have taken poison. But did they take it willingly? Or was it forced down them? We may never know.

DANGEROUS DAYS DEATH IV

POISON

Hemlock is such a nice plant but contains a deadly poison – coniine. Once swallowed in food or drink, the poison rapidly gets to work throughout your body. Not surprisingly, it starts off with the obligatory nausea, abdominal cramps and profuse vomiting.

Rapidly you become confused, agitated and very unsteady on your legs. Sweating like a bull at the beach (posh term: diaphoresis), heart racing, drooling with saliva, you have your first fit. Thrashing around you pee yourself. More fits follow, then, worn out from all the exercise, the poison slows your heart and switches off the part of the brain controlling breathing.

Heart stopped plus not breathing equals double death.
Now if only the poison did that first and avoided all that
mess and pain.

Dr Peter Fox

Did you know ... the elephants of Kush

Elephants were big business in Kush. (Elephants ...
big ... oh, never mind). There is a temple in the Kush
city of Musawwarat es-Sufra (in modern Sudan). It's
a massive complex covering 45,000 square metres.
Everything is on a large scale – doorways, ramps,
courtyards. Why?

One theory is that it was an elephant training camp.
The animals were taken there to be taught how to
perform in battle. The war-elephants were then sold to
Egypt for use in their campaigns.

The only real clue is graffiti showing an elephant
on a ramp.

— COFFIN COMFORTS —

'A sense of humour is good for you. Have you ever
heard of a laughing hyena with heartburn?'

Bob Hope (1903–2003), English-born American comedian

The contents of the tombs tell us a lot about the lives of
the rich Egyptians. They expected to live the afterlife the

way they did this life. They were buried with many of the accoutrements of this life from servants to toilets.

But they knew all about grave-robbers. How could they ensure that they ate well in the next life if their grave grub was pinched? The answer is magical paintings. If you draw a feast on the walls then it will appear in the afterlife.

Mereruka was a vizier to Pharaoh Teti (2345–2333 BC, 6th Dynasty) and he died with enormous wealth. His tomb was greater than that of any commoner in the history of Egypt – 32 rooms. The wall paintings showed him being carried in a chair rather than get dust on his sandals. When he left home there were servants to care for his pet monkey.

He isn't just buried with images of food but with pictures of farmers rearing animals. That makes sense. After Mereruka's grave goodies have passed their sell-by date, he needs those labourers to produce fresh stuff.

They also reveal the tastes of the top table. There are images of antelopes being fed like domesticated beasts. They also show hyenas being force-fed and fattened for the dinner table. Hyenas? No, I'm not having a laugh. A rare delicacy for a great man.*

> 'I will laugh like a hyena, and that when thou art inclined to sleep.'
> William Shakespeare: As You Like It

Hyenas don't do a lot of laughing when they are being eaten.

---

* Hyenas have a bad reputation as scavengers ... though in fact they catch 95 per cent of the food they eat. Superstitions abound – they transport witches, and their body parts are used as ingredients in magic potions. They are accused of robbing graves, and stealing children. In Tanzania hyena faeces are believed to help a child to walk at an early age – so hyena dung is wrapped in their clothes. Hyenas are said to be blood-sucking vampires. Even in the 1800s Greek superstition said they were werewolves who drank the blood of dying soldiers.

— LANDED IN TROUBLE —

> 'Lawyers are like rhinoceroses: thick-skinned,
> short-sighted, and always ready to charge.'
>
> *David Mellor (1949—), British politician*

If you want to make an illicit fortune in Ancient Egypt you didn't have to be a grave-robber. In a long-running legal dispute a man called Neshi had earned a rich estate for his services to Pharaoh Ahmose. Neshi's inheritance split the family and generations went to war with a hundred years of court cases.

But Blood's not thicker than money, as Groucho Marx said. All it needed was a ruthless and devious lawyer to exploit his clients. Even in Ancient Egypt they lurked in the corridors of the court. The ambulance-chaser who was hired by one side was called Khay. First he had a widow and her baby, Mes, evicted from the disputed land – no sentiment there then.

Then Khay's client sought to prove he had a right to own the land – 'After all, I've farmed it for years,' he claimed, when he hadn't. The tax records showed the poor widow had farmed it. Not a problem for Khay. He bribed a court official to forge tax records to show he *had*.

When that baby, Mes, grew up he reopened the case. He knew the tax records had been forged so he simply found witnesses to testify his mother was the rightful owner. He won his case. He also proved Khay was a crooked lawyer. (How can you tell when lawyers are lying? Their lips move.)

Khay was disgraced. Mes was so pleased with his victory in the century-long dispute he had the story inscribed on the walls of his tomb. One of the more unusual epitaphs the world has seen.

Who can blame him? If you can't gloat on your own gravestone then when can you? Scottish outlaw Rob Roy McGregor's name was banned by law, which said that the name McGregor should never be allowed to be heard or seen. His name was inscribed on his tomb with the defiant …

'Despite them.'

PLIGHT OF THE PEASANTS

— UPSTAIRS AND DOWNSTAIRS —

> 'The tyrant is only the slave turned inside out.'
>
> *Egyptian proverb*

Upstairs ...

A Greek visitor to Egypt reported ...

> 'In social meetings among the rich, when the banquet is ended, a servant carries a coffin around the guests. In it there is a wooden image of a corpse, carved and painted to resemble nature as closely as possible. It is about 2 cubits long [almost a metre]. As he shows it to each guest in turn, the servant says, "Gaze here and drink and be merry; for when you die, such will you be."'
>
> *Herodotus*

Cheerful stuff and an echo of the Bible of the time.*

In the temples...

The priests believed in 'perks of the job' and in keeping those perks in the family. Sacrifices? Well, if the gods aren't going to scoff that sacrificial offering it's a shame to see it go to waste ...

> 'The priests enjoy not a few advantages. They consume some of their own property and pay for nothing; every day bread is baked for them with the sacred corn and a plentiful supply of beef and goose flesh is assigned to each. Also a portion of wine made from the grape.†
> They are not allowed to eat fish. Nor do they eat beans, which the priests cannot even bear to look at, since they consider it unclean. Each god has a chief priest; when one dies his son is appointed in his place.'
>
> *Herodotus*

It wasn't all beer and skittles for the powerful priesthood ...

> 'Before offering the sacrifice they fast, and while the bodies of the victims are being roasted they beat themselves.'

---

* The quote 'eat, drink, and be merry' has its origin in the Bible. It comes from Ecclesiastes 8:15. It is also found in Luke 12:19. Neither of these mentions 'for tomorrow we die'. The last was tacked on in modern times from Isaiah 22:13 which says 'let us eat and drink, for tomorrow we die'. Now we know.

† A real luxury. Most Egyptian 'wine' was made from barley as there were no vines in the land. Grape wine would be imported at great expense.

You might say they whip up an appetite. Then again you might not.

... and downstairs

Naturally the life of the Egyptian peasant and slave was not a happy one. It wasn't just the work and hunger, the disease and the dirt. The Egyptians had other quirky and dangerous days to deal with.

🦀 Pharaoh Pepi II (2278–2184 BC) hated flies. His solution was to keep naked slaves nearby and have them smothered in honey to divert the insects from the Pepi person.

🦀 Other members of the privileged classes had luxuries the serving classes could but dream of. In fact YOU, dear reader, would envy one fashion item ... fly swatters made from giraffe tails were a popular accessory in Ancient Egypt.

🦀 Both men and women of the upper classes wore eye make-up called kohl, which was made from an oily mixture. They believed the kohl had magical healing powers – it could restore poor eyesight and fight eye infections.*

🦀 Men and women in Ancient Egypt shaved their heads and often wore wigs. Shaven heads helped them stay cool. Wigs were used as fashion accessories but, as in most societies, their use was perverted to a symbol of

---

* Someone with a crude sense of humour might add that a kohl-mine was a site for sore eyes. I wouldn't dreams of practising such pathetic punning.

status. The rich wore wigs of human hair, the workers wore wigs made from wool or vegetable fibre. Worzel Gummidge would have felt at home in the peasant parlour.

 The lowest class in later dynasties was the swineherd.

> 'Pigs are regarded as unclean animals, so much so that if a man in passing accidentally touch a pig he instantly hurries to the river and plunges in with all his clothes on. Swineherds are forbidden to enter into temples. No one will give their daughter in marriage to a swineherd or take a wife from among them. So they are forced to intermarry among themselves.'
>
> *Herodotus*

— WISE WORDS —

> 'Learn to love books more than you love your mother. There is nothing better than books.'
>
> *The Wisdom of Duauf, an Ancient Egyptian 'Wisdom text'*

The wisdom texts were textbooks for teachers, for children to be taught a particular set of ethics and values. They believed that these texts had been handed down from the gods, and the earliest samples unearthed go back to the Old Kingdom and were for the upper classes.

The wisdom texts were used as schoolboy exercises thousands of years later and by the later kingdoms they took on the tone of a middle-class man talking to his son. Many are relevant today; e.g. Ptahhotep said, 'Never lose your temper, choose your friends carefully … and always be on your best behaviour in someone else's house.'

Impress your friends by citing this ancient wisdom.

The Wisdom of Ptahhotep,*
vizier to King Isesi, 5th Dynasty

- Do not let your heart become proud because of what you know; learn from the ignorant as well as the learned man.

- There are no limits that have been decreed for art; there is no artist who attains entire excellence.

- If you are resolute, acquire a reputation for knowledge and kindliness.

The Wisdom of Amenemope
(8th century BC)

- You can swallow down a fat morsel but you may vomit it up and be emptier than you were before.†

- When you hear things spoken that are of good or evil report, ignore the evil, as though it had never come to your ears.

---

* The named 'authors' of these books were probably not the people who did the writing. The name of a famous person would be added to give the text credibility. In fact they are the first examples of 'ghost-writers'.

† Not literally. 'Swallowing fat' is a metaphor for grabbing at a windfall. 'Spend, spend, spend!' pools winner Viv Nicholson cried in 1961 when she won the equivalent of £3 million today. By 1965 she was bankrupt. She should have had financial advice from Amenemope.

👁 Do not say: 'I have reached a position of power so now I can avenge myself on someone I hate.'

👁 Leave no one behind you at the river crossing while you are lounging in the ferry-boat.

The Wisdom of Pharaoh Kheti
c. 2070 BC (9th Dynasty)

👁 Put not your trust in longevity, a lifetime lasts but a single hour.

👁 Man survives death and a man's actions are heaped at his side. One is faced with the prospect of eternity; the person who makes light of it is an idiot.

👁 Do not exalt someone of noble birth more than you do the child of a humble man, but choose a man because of his actions.

— DEADLY DUTIES —

The Wisdom of Duauf

The book *The Wisdom of Duauf* is an oddity. It is not credited to an eminent sage, but a common man, who has a son called Pepy. The boy has been awarded a scholarship place and is attending a School of Books with the children of the ruling classes. Duauf, like most good dads, is fretting that his son should make the most of this one-off opportunity. He nags Pepy to work hard, pay attention to his teachers, do his homework and become a scribe. That way he can avoid the unpleasant trades open to the unlettered lower classes.

His disdainful summary of the tradesmen's work is exaggerated in order to persuade his son to stick to his studies.* Still the *Wisdom of Duauf* gives us a (slanted) insight into the world of the commoner.

Scribes, wherever they work, will profit. You don't see a stone-worker on an important errand, do you? Or a goldsmith in the rich places a scribe is sent to. But I have seen other professions condemned to drudgery.

- I've seen a coppersmith at his work at the mouth of his furnace. His fingers were like the claws of the crocodile, and he stank more than fish eggs.

- Every carpenter who bears the adze is wearier than a farm labourer. But, unlike the man who labours in the fields, night brings no respite for the carpenter. He must light his lamp and carry on.

- The jeweller pierces hard stone in stringing beads. When he has completed the inlaying of the amulets, his strength vanishes and he is tired out. He sits until sunrise, his knees and his back bent.

- The barber shaves until the end of the evening. But he must be up early, crying out, his bowl upon his arm. He takes himself from street to street to seek out someone to shave. He wears out his arms to fill his belly, like the bee who eats only what he works for.

- The arrow-maker goes north to the Delta to fetch himself reeds for arrows. He must work even while the gnats sting him and the sand fleas bite him.

---

* And still the threat used by today's caring parent: 'Work hard and pass your exams or you'll end up in a dead-end job … like your teacher.'

- The potter is covered with earth as he burrows in the field more than swine to bake his cooking vessels. His clothes are stiff with mud, his head cloth is rags, so he can breathe at his burning furnace. He operates a pestle with his feet, with which he himself is pounded.

- I shall also describe to you the like of the mason-bricklayer. His kidneys are painful because he must be outside in the wind as he lays bricks.

- Opportunities for travel do not exist for the craftsman, for he must remain confined indoors. What he experiences is painful. He has no loincloth. His belt is a cord for his back, a string for his buttocks. His strength has vanished through fatigue and stiffness, kneading all his excrement. He eats bread with his fingers, although he washes himself but once a day.

- The wine-seller carries his shoulder-yoke. Each of his shoulders is burdened with age. A swelling is on his neck, and it festers. So it happens that he sinks down at last and dies from his deliveries more rapidly than one of any other profession.

- The field hand cries out forever. His voice is louder than the raven's. His fingers have become ulcerous with an excess of stench. He is tired out in Delta labour, he is in tatters.

- The weaver inside the weaving house is more wretched than a woman. His knees are drawn up against his belly. He cannot breathe the air. If he wastes a single day without weaving, he is beaten with 50 lashes of the whip. He has to give food to the doorkeeper to allow him to step out into the daylight.

◫ The courier travels abroad after bequeathing his property to his children, being fearful of the lions and the hostile tribes. He only knows himself again when he is back in Egypt. He reaches his household by evening, but the journey has ruined him. There is no happy homecoming.

◫ The furnace-tender, his fingers are foul, the smell thereof is as corpses. His eyes are inflamed because of the heaviness of the smoke. He cannot get rid of his dirt, although he spends the day cutting reeds. Clothes are an abomination to him.

◫ The sandal-maker is utterly wretched carrying his tubs forever. His stores are provided with carcasses, and what he bites is hides.

◫ The washer-man launders at the riverbank in the neighbourhood of the crocodile. His food is mixed with filth, and there is no part of him which is clean. He cleans the clothes of women in menstruation. He weeps when he spends all day with a beating stick and a stone there.

◫ The fowler is utterly afflicted while searching out the birds of the sky. If the flock passes by above him, then he says: 'Would that I might have nets.' But God will not let this come to pass for him, for God is opposed to catching birds.

◫ I mention to you also the fisherman. He is more miserable than any other profession, one who is at his work in a river infested with crocodiles. One did not tell him that a crocodile was standing there, and fear has blinded him.

But if you understand writings, then it will be better for you than any of the professions which I have set before you. A day at school is advantageous to you. Its work is forever.

So one of the more attractive jobs in Ancient Egypt is to be a writer ... a scribe. Yes, it's true there were seven long years of training involved, but the rewards at the end were worth it. Not least among the benefits was the ruling that a writer didn't have to pay taxes.*

— CRIES FROM THE COFFINS —

'Obsessed by a fairy tale, we spend our lives searching for a magic door and a lost kingdom of peace.'

Eugene O'Neill (1888–1953), Irish-American playwright

The oldest death sentence on record was passed in Ancient Egypt in 1500 BC. A teenage male was sentenced to kill himself – by poison or stabbing – for practising magic.

Perhaps he was one of the magicians who wrote magic spells for commoners on their coffins – a privilege only pharaohs had enjoyed in earlier times.

Your corpse will need all the help it can get in the next life. The Egyptians believed that humans possessed a ka, a life-force, which left the body when it died.

In life, the ka had been nourished by food and drink, so it still needed that sustenance after death. Everyone also has a ba, the individual personality. The ba needs to be released from the body so it can team up with the ka. But that can only happen if the body is preserved.

At first the Egyptians claimed that only the pharaoh had a ba. Commoners like you and me faced a bleak, dark

---

* A brilliant idea that we ought to adopt immediately in this modern age. It recognises how much writers suffer for their art, some struggling to get out of bed before noon and come up with 100 words each day. Such a hard life should be recognised. Start a petition at once.

emptiness ... and we didn't like that. Around 2100 BC the Egyptians came to believe that a heavenly home among the stars was available to everyone. And why not? (Well, apart from the fact a 'star' shines due to thermonuclear fusion of hydrogen into helium in its core. The ka-ba-mummy ought, strictly speaking, to be entombed with a very large supply of high-factor sun cream.)

Now this is all very well – equality after death that we never had in life. The problem is, the ka-ba faces a lot of dangers on its journey to the afterlife – the duat. It's a worry, isn't it?

> 'To die, to sleep –
> To sleep, perchance to dream – ay, there's the rub,
> For in that sleep of death what dreams may come.'
>
> *William Shakespeare:* Hamlet

This duat has earthly features like rivers, islands, fields, lakes, hills and caverns, as well as hellish lakes of fire, walls of iron and trees of turquoise. We will have to pass a series of gates guarded by savage spirits – you'll see them as human bodies with grotesque heads of animals, insects, torches or knives.

You will also know them by their names and be able to name them when you meet. Charming and graphic names that need no explanation: 'Blood-drinker who comes from the Slaughterhouse' or 'One who eats the excrement of his hindquarters'.

Get past those guardians of the gates and you will reach your final judgement, known as the 'Weighing of the Heart'. Essentially it is all your childhood Christmas fears revisited when Santa asks: 'Have you been *good*?'

Your evil acts weigh down your heart. So when that heart is weighed in a balance, with a feather on the other side, those wicked deeds will count against you ... the ones you thought you'd got away with.

> 'We have no reliable guarantee that the afterlife will
> be any less exasperating than this one, have we?'
>
> *Noël Coward (1889–1973), English playwright and actor*

The result of these beliefs is that we need all the right prayers to help us in our meeting with the Devourer of Souls and his edible-excrement-eating mates.* You need them inside and outside your coffin, the way the pharaohs had them wrapped inside their bandages or inscribed on the walls of their pyramid tombs.

If you are an ordinary Egyptian, and can afford a coffin, then you need spells every bit as much as a pharaoh … especially if you have a few evil deeds weighing down your heart. Spells that will help you get past the Devourer of Souls, who is looking to snack on your heart if it fails the feather test. Scribes who can paint prayers on your coffin are worth their weight in feathers.

These coffin texts boil down to requests for the guardians of the gates to go easy on you.†

> 'Oh lord of the gods, save me from those who inflict
> wounds, those whose fingers are painful, those who
> instil terror. May their knives not slice into me, may I
> be spared the abattoir and the fiery vats.'
>
> *Coffin Text, 2134 BC*

---

* The Devourer of Souls is part crocodile, part hippopotamus and part lion. It could be a sensation at the local zoo but would probably eat its weight in zookeepers every day.

† We can all be right little pleaders at times, can't we? We plead to the policeman who stops us for speeding. 'Please, officer, I was rushing to see my sick child. Here's my licence. And feel free to keep that tenner tucked inside.'

It was important to know who was guarding the gates. If you didn't know their names then you risked a nasty fate ... even if the guardians looked like alluring females ...

> 'He will arrive at another doorway. He will find the sisterly companions standing there and they will say to him, "Come, we wish to kiss you." And if anyone does not know their names they will cut off his nose and lips.'
>
> *Coffin text, 1782 BC*

Let's hope that, if you *do* get to kiss a sisterly companion, you don't get the one who tucks into the excrement of her hindquarters, eh?

If you could afford it, you could have a scroll known as the Book of the Dead buried with you ... and hope that the guardians of the gates and the gods would take a break from drinking blood to have a quick read. Some of the Book of the Dead claims are the sort most of us could make ...

> Hail, Hept-keht, I have not committed robbery with violence.
> Hail, Am-khaibit, I have not slain men and women.
> Hail, Neha-her, I have not stolen grain.
> Hail, Ruruti, I have not stolen sacrificial offerings from the temples.
> Hail, Basti, I have not eaten the heart.

The guardians and the gods may be just a teensie bit suspicious of some of these Book of the Dead claims (or lies)...

> Hail, Utu-nesert, I have not uttered curses.
> Hail, Her-f-ha-f, I have made none to weep.
> Hail, Maa-antuf, I have not polluted myself.*

And of course the biggest lie of all ...

> Hail, Neba, I have not uttered lies.

If the gods swallowed that lot and more – around 200 prayers – they might let you cross the river of fire, the boiling lake and the snake that spits venom so you reach your promised land.

All of these coffin texts were magical and magic was the province of the priests. Perhaps the executed young man had trodden on temple-dweller toes.

Did you know ... culture shock 1

If the magician was the first recorded death sentence, then the first criminal to be named in Ancient Egyptian history is Mery. But it wasn't for his wealth and power ... it was for tax evasion. Mery would not have been so merry when he was sentenced to 100 blows.

In 2169 BC Pharaoh Kety advised his son that beatings were better than executions...

'Beware of punishing wrongly,' Kety advised his son. 'Do not kill, it will do you no good. Punish with cautions by beatings.'†

---

* And if you don't know what that means, you are too innocent to be reading this book. Put it down at once.
† Just because Kety was ancient and a pharaoh doesn't mean he was right. My old headmaster followed Kety's instructions to the letter and it did me no good. Maybe my headmaster was Kety.

— DANGEROUS DRUGS —

Life in Ancient Egypt was full of the diseases and distresses we all suffer. And there were people willing to relieve you of those discomforts while relieving you of your money. Some have all the efficacy and charm of snake-oil.

Want to avoid unwelcome pregnancy?

> 'A prescription to make a woman cease to become pregnant for one, two or three years.
>
> Grind together a measure of acacia dates with some honey. Moisten seed-wool with the mixture and insert.'
>
> *Medical papyrus*

Many contraceptive measures seemed to involve the insertion of crocodile dung. (Further south in Egypt, elephant dung was recommended as a prophylactic.) Women readers take note: animal droppings as a spermicide may not be effective in itself but it would sure as hell cool the ardour of your lovers ... which will avoid pregnancy. Job done.

> 'Man is more anxious to copulate than a donkey. What restrains him is his purse.'
>
> *Observation of the Scribe Ankhsheshonq*

Some of the medical skills of the Egyptians were as efficacious as eating crusts to give you curly hair. To cure blindness you might (they suggest) like to mash the eye of a pig with honey and red ochre. Pour the concoction into your ear.

Indigestion is caused by evil spirits, so before you drink your medicine you need to recite ...

> 'Come, you who drive out evil things from my stomach and my limbs. He who drinks this shall be cured just as the gods above were cured.'

— DANGEROUS DOCTORS — (AND DENTISTS)

> 'Happiness is your dentist telling you it won't hurt and then having him catch his hand in the drill.'
>
> *Johnny Carson (1925–2005), American TV host and comedian*

Teeth were a problem. The coarse bread wore your dental pegs down and many mummies show signs of tooth-rot that must have been painful in life. Some of the more extreme abscesses probably contributed to their deaths.

So a dentist was an important man. (Unless you were a peasant, in which case you suffered.)

Ankhwa was the first dentist recorded in history. It was a part-time job, you understand – just filling in, as it were. He was Master of the Royal Scribes and Controller of the King's Ship too. But the fact he is listed as Chief Dentist tells us it was a widespread profession.

Some medical treatments were quite advanced for the age. A papyrus dating back to the 1st Dynasty was a detailed guide for medical students. One example, concerning a facial wound, is typical – though you may not fancy it yourself without a full anaesthetic ...

Instructions concerning a wound above the eyebrow

Examination: If thou examinest a man having a wound above his eyebrow, penetrating to the bone, shouldst touch gently his wound, and draw together the gash with stitching.

Diagnosis: Thou shouldst say concerning him: 'One having a wound above his eyebrow. An ailment which I will treat.'

Treatment: Now after thou hast stitched it, thou shouldst bind fresh meat upon it the first day. If thou findest that the stitching of this wound is loose, thou shouldst draw it together for him with two strips of plaster, and thou shouldst treat it with grease and honey every day until he recovers.*

Papyrus textbook of surgery, bought in 1862 by the American
Egyptologist Edwin Smith in Luxor, Egypt

Honey is known to have antimicrobial properties.

The main anaesthetic we know of in Ancient Egypt was opium. Opium poppies were cultivated widely. The sedative properties would be very useful, but the hallucinogenic effects might be pretty unpleasant when a doctor is attempting invasive surgery.

Each case is classified according to one of three verdicts: (1) favourable, (2) uncertain, or (3) unfavourable. The third verdict – expressed in the words, 'an ailment not to be treated' – was the equivalent to today's 'Do not resuscitate'.

---

* You have to hope that the unfortunate patient isn't told he'll have to wait three days for an appointment with the doctor … as 2014 patients are.

Diagnosis: Thou shouldst say regarding him: 'Thou
hast an ailment not to be treated.'

Treatment: Thou shalt not bandage him but fasten him
at his mooring stakes, until the period of his injury
passes by.*

Other not-to-be-treated cases include 'a wound rending
open the brain of his skull'.

Surprisingly, today's doctors agree with the Egyptian
treatment for 'a break in the ribs of his breast'. An ailment
not to be treated.

Some of the techniques suggest a little tact is in order – don't
tell the bloke with the caved-in cranium he is going to die.

*Instructions concerning a gaping wound in his head
penetrating to the bone and perforating the sutures of
his skull.*

Examination: Thou shouldst touch the wound gently,
although he shudders exceedingly. If it is painful for
him to open his mouth and his heart beats feebly, thou
shouldst observe his spittle hanging at his two lips and
not falling off, while he discharges blood from both his
nostrils and from both his ears; he suffers with stiffness
in his neck, and is unable to look at his two shoulders
and his breast.

First diagnosis: Thou shouldst say regarding him: 'This
is an ailment with which I will contend.'†

---

* Euphemism for: Tie him to the bed till he recovers or dies.
† You don't have to be an Egyptian doctor to know this man is a goner.
'I will contend' with your wound is not the same as saying, 'I will cure

First treatment: Now as soon as thou findest that the ligaments of that man's jaw have contracted, thou shouldst have made for him something hot until he is comfortable, so that his mouth opens. Thou shouldst bind it with grease, honey and lint, until thou knowest that he has reached a decisive point.

Doctors are advised to resort to magic in only one case out of the 48 cures recorded.

Examination: If thou examinest a man having a wound in his forehead, smashing the shell of his head.

Treatment: Thou shouldst prepare for him the egg of an ostrich, ground to a powder with grease and placed in the opening of his wound. Now prepare for him the egg of an ostrich, ground to a powder and made into poultices for drying up that wound. Thou shouldst apply and uncover it the third day, and find it knitting together the shell, the colour being like the egg of an ostrich.

That which is to be said as a charm over this recipe: 'Repelled is the enemy that is in the wound. The evil that is in the blood is cast out. I am under the protection of Isis; my rescue is the son of Osiris.'

Now afterwards thou shouldst cool it for him with a compress of figs, grease, and honey, cooked and cooled, and applied to it.

---

this wound.' But if he's had his skull smashed he won't notice the subtle difference.

Other symptoms are captured by delightful phrases like …

> 'The odour of the breath is like the urine of sheep.'

The medical profession was a profitable one. Hesira the Dentist was able to have a fine tomb built for himself. Among the wall paintings, the carved chests and rich vases there are board games. Hesira couldn't keep the draughts out of his tomb.

Once bitten

During the 12th Dynasty (1991–1878 BC) an expedition set out to the south-west of Sinai to bring back precious stones from the turquoise terraces. There were stone-cutters and quarrymen along with cup-bearers to keep them supplied with water. They even took their own priest. But a key member of the expedition was the 'Scorpion Doctor'. No, he wasn't there to treat sick scorpions – his job was to cure workers who were stung.* As if rockfalls and the fierce heat weren't enough to contend with, the poisonous creatures were a major hazard.

---

* This was a specialist area of Egyptian medicine. A skilled scorpion doctor like Wennefer in the reign of Nectanebo II (360–342 BC) rose to the very top of the tree and won rich rewards as well as a fine funerary monument from the pharaoh. All for curing scorpion bites. Was his choice of funeral music, 'I'd like to teach the world to sting'?

DANGEROUS DAYS DEATH V

SCORPION BITES

The scorpion's tail whips over, the hypodermic-like stinger puncturing your skin with a quick, sharp pain. The venom rapidly causes an extreme burning sensation in your skin as the area swells and becomes red. More worryingly, the venom spreads through the bloodstream affecting nerves and muscles throughout the body. Horrendous, painful cramps start doubling you up as patchy numbness appears anywhere. Other areas of skin become very sensitive and painful, like a series of severe electric shocks. Crying and screaming, writhing around in excruciating pain, you start to profusely sweat, vomit and drool saliva. Men also get sustained erections, priapism, but their mind is on other things and a drooling vomiter is not that alluring, mostly. The venom also affects your heart, causing it to beat irregularly and then finally stop.

Dr Peter Fox

Horwerra boasted of a trouble-free expedition.

'I made my expedition very well. There were no raised voices against the labour and what I did was successful.'

Horwerra inscription at the Sinai Turquoise mine

But, like the scorpion, there was a sting in the tale. He was telling a little fib about the happy band of loyal workers. The truth is Horwerra faced a revolt among his workers, who told him it was madness to mine in the furnace of a Sinai summer and that the turquoise would be damaged by the fierce sun.

He persuaded the workers that they were doing this for the glory of the king, Amenemhet III. The workers backed down and Horwerra brought all 23 home safe with the help of the doctor.

— DEADLY DAUGHTERS —

> 'Adults are obsolete children.'
>
> *Dr Seuss (1904–91), American writer*

Except, Dr Seuss, obsolete machines are sent to a scrapyard. Care for the elderly is a problem as old as the pyramids.

Ctesicles was an Egyptian who was obliged to petition the king against his uncaring daughter, Nicē.* Echoes of today can be heard …

> To King Ptolemy
>
> Greetings from Ctesicles. I am being wronged by Dionysius and my daughter Nicē. For though I have nurtured her, being my own daughter, and educated her and brought her up to womanhood, when I was stricken with bodily infirmity and my eyesight enfeebled she would not furnish me with any of the necessaries of life. And when I wished to obtain justice from her in Alexandria, she begged my pardon and in year 18 she gave me in the temple of Arsinoe Actia a written oath by the king that she would pay me 20 drachmae every month.
>
> Now, however, corrupted by Dionysius, who is a comedian, she is not keeping any of her commitments to me, in contempt of my old age and my present infirmity.

---

* An ironic name if ever there was one.

> I beg you therefore, O king, not to suffer me to be wronged by my daughter and Dionysius the comedian who has corrupted her, but to let your judges summon them and hear our case; and if my words are true, let your judges deal with her corrupter as seems good to him and compel my daughter Nicē to yield me my rights.'
>
> *Ctesicles (an Egyptian, probably living at Crocodilopolis),*
> *Petition 220 BC*

One hopes the 'comedian' had the smile wiped off his face.

As King Lear would complain in the timeless verse of Shakespeare, 'How sharper than a serpent's tooth it is to have a thankless child!'

— THE LAW'S LONG ARM —

It wasn't all oppression for the peasantry. Horemheb was an army general who seized power from the failing 18th Dynasty to form the 19th. He was desperate to have the peasantry on his side so he enacted laws to help them.

> 'His majesty commands that if any officer is guilty of theft or extortion against the poor then the law shall be enacted against the officer. His nose shall be cut off.'
>
> *Horemheb law, 1315 BC*

A punishment not to be sniffed at. Horemheb said that any peasant who was robbed could be excused paying his taxes. Tax collectors were to have their powers controlled. That would have gone down well with Egyptian peasants, as it would with today's peasants like you and me.

Any soldiers who bullied and looted the peasantry would be punished ...

> 'He that goeth about stealing hides shall have the law executed against him. He shall be beaten by a hundred blows, opening five wounds, and taking from him the hides he stole.'

No hiding place for the looter then.

Pharaoh Seti was concerned about stealing from the gods. His conquered territories in Nubia were dedicated to the gods. Stealing the livestock or thieving from the properties in Nubia was a more severe crime than doing the same in Egypt. It was stealing from the gods. Any Egyptian who purloined the gods' goods was to be severely punished ...

> 'Punishment shall be done to him with two hundred blows and five open wounds.
>
> For any high officer who offends, punishment shall be done to him by cutting off his ears.
>
> And for the cattle herdsman who sells the gods' cattle, punishment shall be done by casting him down and impaling him on a stake.'
>
> *Laws of Seti I (1280 BC)*

Count Vlad Dracula was famous for lowering victims onto the sharp point of a stake so it entered the body via the rectum. Death was slow and an entertainment in the dining halls of his Transylvanian palaces. But in Egypt the 'casting down' seems to suggest the victim was thrown from a height onto the point of the stake. A quicker death. Maybe.

— DOMESTIC DANGER —

'It's only in love and in murder that we still remain sincere.'

Friedrich Dürrenmatt (1921–90), Swiss author

A cache of papyri were found in the tomb of the vizier Ipi from the Middle Kingdom. They included personal letters written by a wealthy priest, Heqanakht, to his family.

It seems Heqanakht was obliged to stay near the temple in Thebes while his family lived on his farm many miles away. The letters home are fretful and constantly complaining about the family's lives in his absence.

'Take great care. Watch over my seed corn. Look after my property. I hold you responsible for it. Take great care with all my property.'*

Heqanakht papyri

When the price of barley rose he was happy to cut his family's ration and sell their dinners to make a profit. This was not a lovable man. But it was when sex reared its cobra head that things turned really nasty. Heqanakht's concubine was parachuted into his home and proved as popular as a slug in your lunch-box salad.

Heqanakht had to write and order the family and staff to treat her with respect. One of the maidservants was especially spiteful and was given the boot … or the sandal (with a steel toecap).

---

* Doesn't he go on … and on. The temptation must have been to reply, 'Yes, Heqanakht, we get the message.'

The tensions were so dramatic an archaeologist's wife adapted the situation into a murder-mystery novel. The writer's name was Agatha Christie and the book is called *Death Comes as the End*. The unpopular concubine is the first victim and one by one the family are bumped off (till it is obvious that the butler did it).

Four thousand years later Heqanakht is still a recognisable character – and his family tensions still a motive for murder.

— A WOMAN'S PLACE —

> 'The trouble with some women is that they get all excited about nothing – and then marry him.'
>
> *Cher (1946—), American singer/actress*

The woman's life was as tough in Egypt as it has always been in history.

Cleaning

There was advice for women written on papyrus documents, which is odd because most women couldn't read. But you can read and may appreciate this advice …

> 'To expel fleas from the house, sprinkle it with natron salt in water until they pass away.
>
> To prevent mice approaching, fat of cat is placed on all things.
>
> To prevent a serpent from coming out of its hole a bulb of onion is placed in the opening of the hole and it will not come out.'
>
> *Ebers medical papyrus*

Insect repellent was made from 'oriole fat', but those flies must have been a nuisance as a lot of householders couldn't be bothered to take rubbish to the local tip or the river. They threw it onto the street. The ground level rose from year to year.

Washing

Women were proud of keeping their clothes a dazzling white but it was hard labour. On wash day they took their clothes to the river, applied natron soap and pounded the clothes with a wooden paddle. Those who could afford it used a washerman who offered a door-to-door service. By the Middle Kingdom these tradesmen were using hot water to get deep-down clean.

Cooking

Ovens were often on the flat roofs of the houses and with lack of refrigeration it was a constant battle to supply the family table. Families could keep their own ducks and geese, sheep and goats. Best not to get too attached to next week's dinner though.

Birds could be caught in nets and didn't need refrigeration. Just pop them into a cage and fatten them up until you are ready to wring their necks.

Fruit and veg seemed to provide a regular five-a-day. So much so that the Israelites who were expelled from Egypt bemoaned their loss.

> 'Will no one give us meat? Think of it. In Egypt we had fish for the asking, cucumbers and watermelons, leeks and onions and garlic. Now our throats are parched; there is nothing wherever we look, except this manna.'*

---

* By manna they probably meant the excretion of small insects onto tamarind sticks. A tasty treat still appreciated by modern-day Bedouins. Why were the Israelites complaining?

Drink

Women held their own in drinking at parties. There are painted scenes of women being drunk and publicly sick. In the tomb of Paheri there is an image of a woman demanding drink from a waiter ...

> 'Give me eighteen cups of wine. My throat is dry as straw and I want to drink till I am drunk.'

Eighteen cups of wine ought to do it then.

Loose women

If a man strayed from his wife then the other woman was often blamed. She was a temptress who had taken advantage of the poor man's weakness to satisfy her wicked desires. But these warnings were all written by men, so of course there's bound to be that sort of distortion of the truth.

A typical tale tells how a woman led a helpless man into her snare ...

> Then she spoke to him saying, 'You are very strong. I see your vigour every day.' And she desired to know him as a man. She got up, took hold of him and said, 'Come, let us spend an hour lying in bed together. It will be good for you. And afterwards I shall make you some fine new clothes.'
>
> *Egyptian text: 'Tale of Two Brothers'*

And she didn't even offer to take crocodile dung precautions. Shameless.

It was a dangerous thing for a wife to be caught in adultery. The husband was entitled to inflict fierce physical punishment. In the Old Kingdom of Cheops there is a story of an unfaithful wife being burned and having her ashes scattered on the Nile.

A tale (maybe based on fact) tells of a straying woman being killed and fed to dogs so she couldn't enjoy the afterlife. Roman historian Diodorus Siculus wrote that an unfaithful Egyptian wife was liable to have her nose cut off. (Her lover would get away with a beating. How fair is that?)

Children

> 'There can be no keener revelation of a society's soul than the way in which it treats its children.'
>
> *Nelson Mandela (1918–2013), South African president*

In the afterlife there was a lot of rumpy-pumpy, judging from the grave goods. Female fertility dolls – with wide hips – were common. Men were buried with false penises moulded onto their mummy. One Egyptian army captain in the 11th Dynasty made a rather exaggerated boast of his sexual prowess when he said…

> 'I have fathered 70 children, all the issue of one wife.'

A touch unlikely, don't you think? But children were seen as proof of virility and a large family was seen as a blessing too. Sterile men were known to kill themselves in shame at being unable to father a child.

There was advice on how to treat children which is still valid today ...

> 'Do not prefer one child above the others; after all you never know which of them will be kind to you.'
>
> *Advice from Late Period Egypt*

Once a child was on the way the parents were usually eager to know the gender before it was born. There was a simple test; sprinkle the woman's urine on a patch of growing wheat and barley – if the barley shoots up, it's a boy.

Sadly, death in childbirth was a constant danger. The Egyptians turned away from the doctors at that point and put their faith in prayer.

— HISTORY OF HERODOTUS —

> 'The Egyptians are religious to excess, far beyond any other race of men. Their manners and customs are the exact reverse of the common practice of mankind.'
>
> *Herodotus*

Herodotus made extensive notes for our benefit. He was a bit gullible – some of the things the natives told him were untrue but he swallowed them.

But no historian is perfect. He can only report what he hears and sees.

> 'History, a distillation of rumour.'
>
> *Thomas Carlyle (1795–1881), Scottish philosopher*

He was also a bit of a Greek snob.

His insights into Egyptian life are still worth reading …

1   The Egyptians were into nit control.

'In other countries the priests have long hair. In Egypt
their heads are shaven so that no lice may adhere to
them when they are in the service of the gods.'

2   The Egyptians were not into food hygiene.

'They knead their dough with their feet, but they mix
mud and even take up dirt.'

3   The Egyptians were into detox.

'For three successive days in each month they purge
their bodies by means of emetics which they do for
their health.'

4   The Egyptians were into sushi.

'Many kinds of fish they eat raw, either salted or dried
in the sun.'*

5   The Egyptians were into washing up.

'They drink out of bronze cups which they scour every
day; there is no exception to this practice.'

6   The Egyptians were into pets.

'If a cat dies in a private house of natural causes all the
inmates shave their eyebrows. On the death of a dog
they shave their head and whole bodies. The cats are
embalmed and buried in sacred places.'

---

* Vegetarians look away now. They also ate quails, ducks and small birds
raw.

⌁ THE CULT OF THE CATS ⌁

'I had been told that the training procedure with cats was difficult. It's not. Mine had me trained in two days.'

Bill Dana (1924—), American comedian,

One of the most popular cults to arise in Late Period Egypt was that of the cat goddess Bast. The thinking was that cats were the natural enemies of the rats and mice that ate the grain that kept the humans alive. Cats were even known to combat deadly snakes such as cobras. They were revered and valued.✱

Cats of the royal palaces could be dressed in golden jewellery and were allowed to eat from their owners' plates. 'How cool! A cult for cats,' the ailurophiles cry.

Were these felicitous felines fed on fillet steaks, pampered and provided with toilet trays of lavender litter and allowed to lap the coolest cream?

No. These were the most dangerous days in cat history. It was the tourist trade that threatened their nine lives of luxury. Many thousands of moggies were mummified for sale to Bast pilgrims, who presented them to the goddess as an offering.

But these weren't gently passed-away pussies. X-rays show that the cats were often killed by having their necks broken. The bodies were dried out using Natron salt, exactly like human mummies.

✱ The moggies have had their moments in history. Dick Whittington's cat was the making of him … or her – we've all seen the pantomime and wondered how a bloke in thigh-slapping tights ever made Lord Mayor of London.

They were then extravagantly wrapped with the forelegs lying down the front and the back legs drawn up behind.

The main centre for the cult of Bast was at the town of Bubastis on the Nile Delta. Vast graveyards have been discovered; in 1888, a farmer uncovered a plot of many hundreds of thousands of these mummified cat corpses. Cruellest of all, it seems probable that the animals were specially bred to die for the cult. (A vegetarian may say that's a bit like breeding adorable fluffy lambs and cute calves to eat.)

— TEEN TANTRUM —

Teenagers, eh? It's the hormones that make them cranky. Were they as stroppy in Ancient Egypt? You bet. If you've ever known of a teenager who demanded a guitar from a parent then you will recognise the sarcastic tone of Theon 2,000 years ago …

> Father.
>
> Oh thanks for not taking me to the city. If you won't take me with you to Alexandria I won't write to you, or speak to you or say goodbye to you. And if you go to Alexandria I won't shake your hand or ever greet you again. That's what'll happen if you won't take me. Mum said to her friend, 'He's quite upset at being left behind.'
>
> Yes, it was good of you to send me a present on the day you sailed. But I want a lyre. Send me a lyre, *please*, or I won't eat and I won't drink. So there!
>
> Theon
>
> *Letter from Theon to his father*

Sound familiar?

GREED OF THE GREEKS

— ALEXANDER THE GRAPE —

> 'A tomb now suffices him for whom the world was
> not enough.'
>
> *Alexander the Great's epitaph*

In 356 BC, Alexander the Great was born in Macedonia – north of Greece. He would go on to conquer the crumbling empires of Persia, Mesopotamia and, in 332 BC, Egypt. The Persians had ruled Egypt for four years and were as popular as ants at a picnic. Alexander was hailed as a saviour, a god, a pharaoh.

He made himself pharaoh and endeared himself to the native Egyptians by founding a new city on the Nile delta – Alexandria. Then he rode off into the sunset. He was restless and (allegedly) complained …

> 'There are no more worlds to conquer!'
>
> *Alexander the Great (356–323 BC)*

His invasion of India was a bit of an embarrassment. His soldiers refused to go any further and he had to turn back.

He retraced his conquering steps to Babylon – planning to make it his new capital – and died. Was it simply an excess of wine that killed him? Or was he poisoned?

One theory concerns a disgraced viceroy, Antipater. This man had been summoned to Babylon to meet Alexander. He must have feared execution. As it happens, Antipater's son was Alexander's wine-bearer. Who better to poison the tyrant's tipple? He wouldn't be the first, or the last, ruler of Egypt to suffer that fate.

Pharaoh Alexander's mummification was unconventional. His body was placed in a gold sarcophagus that was then filled with honey to preserve it. (Parting is such sweet sorrow, Alex.)

While the obese empire of Alexander was being fought over like jackals scrapping over the corpse of a lion king, his gold-encased corpse set off on an adventurous life of its own.

❀ It was sent back to Alexander's Macedonian home for burial but hijacked by Ptolemy – one of Alexander's generals who had been installed on the throne of Egypt.

❀ The coffin was taken to Memphis (20 miles south of Cairo) and placed in a tomb. Rest in peace, Alex? No ...

❀ Ptolemy IX (143–81 BC) placed the corpse in a glass coffin. So that admirers could see the heroic Alex, you ask? No. So the greedy Greek could melt down the gold coffin for coins.

❀ Roman rulers Julius Caesar and Augustus Caesar both visited the tomb to pay homage. It is said Augustus accidentally knocked off Alexander's nose.

⚙ Roman Emperor Caligula stole Alexander's breastplate for his own use – delusions of grandeur, no doubt.

⚙ Emperor Caracalla (reigned 198–211) visited the tomb and after that its fate is unknown.

The chosen satrap, Ptolemy, didn't want to rule like some school prefect under the control of a Council of State that ruled Alexander's empire. He wanted to be headmaster of his own domain. He needed a symbol of power. Forget crowns, sceptres and orbs. Ptolemy wanted the corpse of Alexander.

Ptolemy's troops kidnapped the coffin as it was on the road back to Greece. 'Alexander wanted to be buried in Egypt,' Ptolemy declared. The corpse-snatchers made their way back to Egypt and regent Perdiccas attacked. An attack on a funeral procession is not the sort of thing we expect to see today. But Ptolemy defeated the Greeks and took Alex back to Egypt.*

General Ptolemy consolidated his position by having himself anointed 'pharaoh'. We don't know if that's what Alexander wanted. On his deathbed he was asked who should succeed him and he purportedly answered, 'The strongest'.

Nominally the empire was ruled by Alex's posthumously born baby, Alexander IV, and his feeble-minded half-brother Philip III. Of course it all ended badly. Philip's feeble mind hit the ground on 25 December 317 BC when he was executed and his wife was forced to commit suicide.† Have yourself a very merry Christmas.

---

* Meanwhile Perdiccas was murdered by his own officers. Losing the battle was bad enough. Being butchered by your own men is rubbing salt into the wound … or wounds, in Perdiccas's case.

† On the orders of Alexander the Great's mother, Olympias. That woman was deadlier than a land mine. You'll be relieved to hear she was captured and executed by friends of the people she'd murdered. She was denied a proper burial. As popular as bubonic plague.

Alexander IV lived on a little longer. Inevitably he was assassinated. He was only 12 years old.* Dangerous days indeed.

Did you know ... culture shock 2

In Egypt, children were perceived as a blessing. The Greeks who sometimes left unwanted infants (usually girls) outdoors to die, were amazed to discover that the Egyptians did not.

Egypt, meanwhile, was in the grip of its last dynasty. The Greek Ptolemy family.

THE PTERRIBLE PTOLEMIES

'Bernard of Chartres used to compare us to puny dwarfs perched on the shoulders of giants. He pointed out that we see more and farther than our predecessors, not because we have keener vision or greater height, but because we are lifted up and borne aloft on their gigantic stature.'

John of Salisbury (1120–80), English author

---

* The orders went out from Alexander's rivals: 'Poison the prince and his mother secretly.' The order was half obeyed – the two died, but it was hardly a secret as you are reading about it over 2,000 years later. Someone talked. They always do.

Alexander the Great had invaded Egypt in 332 BC on his way to Alexandrian greatness and an early grave. Up like a rocket, down like a stick was young Alex. His influence on Egypt was lasting. The Greeks would rule for 300 years, making the peasants poorer and their foreign royals richer.

Alexander had restored many of the antiquities that had made Egypt great. But at the same time Egypt ceased to be the hidden jewellery box of the world. It was part of the Mediterranean world now. A land rife for exploitation by the biggest bruisers who bullied their way through the empires of Europe. From the Roman Empire to the British Empire, Egypt would be merely a commodity.

Its rulers were no longer gods. Ptolemy I was fighting for his life against his co-inheritors of the Alexander Empire. He was forced to leave a locum to rule Egypt: Cleomenes.

Cleomenes used the chance to exploit the people, rob the temples and even purloin the pay of the soldiers. He was going to make the most of this opportunity to live the high life, no matter who was hurt in the process.

'*Dum vivimus vivamus.*'
(While we are alive, let us live.)

Latin proverb

Ptolemy had to have Cleomenes executed.

Despite the foreign rulers and their Greek ways, Egypt kept its strong priesthood – a civil service that was stable and efficient. The country adopted the Ptolemy royal family as its own. It was business as usual. And that meant dangerous days for those at the top.

— PTOLEMY II —
(285–246 BC)

Ptolemy's son succeeded peacefully but his queen, Arsinoe, was suspected of treason, so she and their children were banished to Southern Egypt. Needing a wife he could trust, Ptolemy married his sister.*

— PTOLEMY III —
(246–222 BC)

The young warrior king took the throne and charged off with an army to Syria to help his sister, Berenice, in distress. Before he could get there, Berenice was murdered along with her son. Ptolemy avenged her by sacking the city. Egypt was a force to fear under his rule.

— PTOLEMY IV —
(222–205 BC)

'It is forbidden to kill; therefore all murderers are punished unless they kill in large numbers and to the sound of trumpets.'

Voltaire (1694–1778), French writer, historian and philosopher

Ptolemy IV was the black sheep of the family. His friend and mentor was the distinctly dodgy Sosibius, whose word

---

* And to avoid any confusion among the tabloid press and gossip magazines she was called Arsinoe too ... or Arsinoe Two, if you like.

was law. It was probably the seedy Sosibius who started the rumour that Ptolemy IV's mother and brother were plotting against him. His mother was murdered by poison and younger brother scalded to death. Nasty.

Ptolemy's 'favourites' included his mistress Agathoclea, who ran the country while encouraging the pharaoh to enjoy his dissolute pleasures.

The pharaoh was present at the Battle of Raphia where Egypt won a brilliant victory and secured her empire. This is the only known battle in which African and Asian elephants were used against each other. Ptolemy's elephants were African elephants while the Syrian enemy used Asian elephants, brought from India. It seems the African elephants could not bear the smell, sound and sight of their Indian cousins and were reluctant warriors. They packed their trunks and said goodbye to the struggle – running backwards through their own troops.

The war victories of Ptolemy IV might have been great, but the costs in tax and the neglected administration of the country were ruinous.

His sister, Arsinoe, was probably relieved when he died in 204 BC, aged 41. His excesses killed him. But Arsinoe never got to hear that she had become a merry widow. The news was withheld from her. The heir was her infant son Ptolemy V. The pharaoh's favourites, Agathoclea and her brother Agathocles, had Arsinoe poisoned before she could assume the role of her son's guardian.*

---

* If she had news of her husband–brother's death then she may have been forewarned and a bit more careful about what she drank. Poison seemed to flow like milk in a dairy in Ptolemaic Egypt.

～ PTOLEMY V ～
(205–180 BC)

> 'You cannot run with the hare and hunt with the hounds.'
>
> *English idiom*

Ptolemy V was only five years old, so it was natural that Agathoclea and Agathocles would claim to be his regents and run the country on his behalf.

The mob of Alexandria begged to disagree. They broke into the palace and lynched the sneaky siblings. Ptolemy V was to remain the puppet of other royal guardians – no better than Agathoclea and Agathocles – and they simply watched over the decline of the empire, whittled away by rebels within and invaders without. The Syrians and Macedonians ganged up to begin nibbling away at the fringes of the Egyptian Empire.

In a desperate bid to bring peace, Ptolemy V eventually married Cleopatra I, the daughter of his Syrian enemy. (Their son would become Ptolemy VI.) Ptolemy V grew into a keen athlete and hunter. His diplomacy was true to his lifestyle – he ran with the hare and hunted with the hounds. When Rome went to war with his Syrian father-in-law, the ptreacherous Ptolemy sided with the Romans.

The rebels in the south had broken away under their own pharaohs, Hugronaphor and Ankhmakis. Eventually they made peace and Ptolemy guaranteed their safety, swearing upon his honour as a pharaoh. Of course he reneged on that promise and had them put to death with immense cruelty. Never ptrust a Ptolemy.

— PTOLEMY VI —
(180–145 BC)

When Ptolemy V died, history repeated itself. Ptolemy VI was just entering his teens so his mother appointed herself as guardian. When she died, two courtiers took the reins.

They went for glory to enhance their status. They declared war on Syria and were duly defeated. Ptolemy VI married his sister, Cleopatra II, and they had four children. It was his brother, Ptolemy VIII, who let the family down by briefly replacing Ptolemy VI on the throne.

There was a worrying peek into the future in 170 BC when Antiochus IV invaded Egypt twice. He was crowned as its king in 168, but abandoned his claim on the orders of the Roman Senate. So the rising force that was Rome was showing an interest in Egypt. Like the Terminator, they'd be back – and it would be terminal.

Ptolemy's respite was brief and it all ended in tears. In 145 BC he died of battle wounds received against Alexander Balas of Syria.

Did you know … the elephants forget

A Jew called Dositheus plotted to murder Ptolemy IV in his sleep, but failed. Ptolemy wanted revenge and after winning the battle of Raphia he visited Jerusalem and declared that he would enter the Temple. God, miffed at not being consulted, struck down the pharaoh – probably with a thunderbolt gun set to stun – and Ptolemy fell to the ground. Now he too was miffed.

God (and the Jews) needed to be taught a lesson. When Ptolemy IV returned to Alexandria he gathered all the Jews of Alexandria and Egypt, had them bound and dragged into the arena. Their punishment was to be trampled by elephants. God, however, was not in the mood to be defied. One trunk call was all it took. The beasts threw themselves upon the pharaoh's troops instead.

— PTOLEMY VIII —
(170–118 BC)

> 'Murder's out of tune,
> And sweet revenge grows harsh.'
>
> *William Shakespeare:* Othello

What is it about the number VIII? Henry VIII was an obese, ruthless psychopath. Ptolemy VIII was an obese, ruthless psychopath.

Ptolemy VI had had help from his son Ptolemy VII as co-ruler, but dastardly Uncle Ptolemy VIII married Cleopatra II. She produced a son for Ptolemy VIII so Ptolemy VII was redundant. Step-dad and Uncle Ptolemy VIII had him murdered.* The murder was committed during the wedding feast.

This Ptolemy was nicknamed 'Phsycon' – pot-bellied or sausage-belly. 'Psycho' would have been equally appropriate.

Now if you think the pharaohs were an incestuous bunch, they were about to get even more twisted in their relationships.

---

* There were so many Ptolemies around, the ancient historians became mightily confused.

Ptolemy VIII fancied Cleopatra II's daughter, Cleopatra III. He proposed a 'liaison'. She said, 'Yes, if you'll make me joint ruler.' He agreed, and began ruling with two queens, mother and daughter. Sleeping arrangements must have been interesting.

Even the Egyptians, used to a cosy brother–sister marriage, were angry. They were fans of Cleopatra the Mother. Ptolemy VIII decided a holiday was in order and went off to Cyprus, taking Cleo II the daughter ... or they 'fled' if we are being honest. A wise move, as he left just as a mob broke into the palace to turn sausage-belly into sausage-meat.

He had also aroused anger by his purge against intellectuals in Alexandria.

> 'He expelled all intellectuals: philologists,
> philosophers, professors of geometry, musicians,
> painters, schoolteachers and physicians.'*
>
> *Menecles of Barca, Libyan historian*

Cleopatra the Mother ruled with the blessing of the mob. Ptolemy VIII's revenge was so brutal even Henry VIII wouldn't have contemplated it. He took his 12-year-old son by Cleopatra the Mother and dismembered him. He sent the bits to her. He timed the delivery to arrive on her birthday.

In 129 BC the murderous Phsycon returned and Cleopatra the Mother fled to Syria. Phsycon died in 116 BC and left the throne to Cleopatra III, plus whichever son she wanted as co-regent.

---

* Echoes from the distant past of our own age. From 1975 to 1979 in Cambodia books were burned, teachers, merchants and almost the entire intellectual elite of the country were murdered to clear the way for agricultural communism. Mass graves became known as 'the Killing Fields'. The murderous regime was led by the psychopath Pol Pot – a former history teacher. Say no more.

～ PTOLEMY IX and X ～
(116–80 BC)

Curiously, the Egyptians refused to accept Cleopatra's choice of son, Ptolemy X, and forced her to select her older son, Ptolemy IX, to rule jointly. The days of the all-powerful pharaohs were slipping away and democracy was rearing its handsome head.

The unfavoured son, Ptolemy IX, accused of plotting to kill his mum, Cleopatra III, ran off into exile. That may have been a false charge devised by Mum to leave the coast clear for favoured son Ptolemy X. If so, it worked a treat. Mother and younger son ruled jointly.

But Cleo III grew tired of favoured son Ptolemy X and drove him into exile, too. Then she made a fatal mistake – they usually do. In 101 BC, the prodigal Ptolemy X returned under the pretence of a reconciliation with his mother. Once he was back, he duly had her assassinated. What goes around comes around, Cleo. Her hands were so steeped in blood and treachery she may have smiled a wry smile as she died and muttered, 'I shoulda known better.'

Ptolemy X ruled a while but was eventually driven out of Egypt after selling off Alexander the Great's gold coffin to raise money. He bequeathed his kingdom to Rome in his will, though he stipulated that they could not claim their inheritance while he was still alive. What the will did do was secure him credit with moneylenders in Rome. This allowed him to finance a fleet – which did him little good. He was killed in a naval battle off Cyprus.

⁓ PTOLEMY XI ⁓
(80 BC),

⁓ PTOLEMY XII ⁓
(80–58 BC and 55–51 BC) and

⁓ BERENICE IV ⁓
(59–55 BC)

There were no direct male Ptolemy heirs so the throne went to Queen Berenice. A male was needed for the sake of appearances so she married her young nephew Ptolemy XI. The ungrateful lad didn't like his new wife so he had her murdered. Again the mob had other ideas and he became next in the line of lynched rulers.

Ptolemy XII was an illegitimate son of the dynasty. On the up side he had the support of the Mediterranean super-power, Rome. On the down side he had the support of the Mediterranean super-power, Rome. That made him a target for the Egyptian nationalists. He fled to Rome to seek succour from his chums.

Meanwhile his daughter, Berenice IV, took the throne and ruled with her mother. A year later Berenice had her mother murdered. Typical. The council were not sure a 21-year-old could do the job alone, so they forced her to marry a Syrian cousin, Seleucus, the token male. Perhaps he upset her. Perhaps it was something he said. Their marriage lasted a week before she had him strangled. Sorry, Seleucus, but you know what they say …

'They are not long, the days of wine and roses:
Out of a misty dream
Our path emerges for a while, then closes
Within a dream.'

Ernest Dowson (1867–1900), English poet

After three years her father, Ptolemy XII, returned from Roman exile with an army of his Roman friends ... well, they were 'friends' because he bribed them with the promise of Egyptian riches.

Berenice was imprisoned and murdered – beheaded. It's hard to feel sorry for these Valkyries.

The dangerous days of the pharaohs were as bloody as ever. But they were almost over.

Now the throne was taken by the last – and most notorious – of the Ptolemy Dynasty. She wasn't as ruthless and bloodthirsty as some of her predecessors, but her story was more dramatic. And so she is remembered.

THE CULT OF CLEOPATRA

— CLEOPATRA VII —
(69 BC–30 BC)

> 'Age cannot wither her, nor custom stale
> Her infinite variety.'
>
> *William Shakespeare:* Antony and Cleopatra

> 'How different, how very different, from the home life
> of our own dear queen.'
>
> *Anonymous Victorian critique of*
> *Sarah Bernhardt's performance in* Cleopatra*

The Ptolemy family had ruled, as an occupying regime, for 300 years.

But it was the last of the line who grabbed all the historical headlines.

King Richard III of England reigned for a couple of forgettable years. Yet he is remembered because Will Shakespeare wrote a play about him. And people remember Shakespeare's fiction.

---

* Sarah, as a slightly OTT Cleopatra, smashed pots and tore down curtains in her rage at her Antony's infidelity. Sadly, how very sadly, this memorable quote from an audience member is probably apocryphal. Is there nothing sacred in this world?

The Bard did the same for Cleopatra. A queen who ruled for 30 turbulent years to become the most memorable name in Egyptian history.* Hers was a love story – rather a sordid one at times, but dramatic enough to fill a chick-lit book or two. She is remembered for Antony and her asp, just as King Alfred is for his burned cakes, King Canute for his wet feet, or Queen Victoria for her unamused scowl. Somewhere in the myths the truth lies tangled.

> 'The good ended happily, and the bad unhappily. That is what fiction means.'
>
> *Oscar Wilde*

What are those truths? I'm glad you asked.

· 1 ·

> MARK ANTONY: 'Hello – there is news from Egypt, Ptolemy is trying to usurp Cleopatra.'
>
> JULIUS CAESAR: 'Trying to do what with her?'
>
> MARK ANTONY: 'Usurp her.'
>
> JULIUS CAESAR: 'Sounds positively revolting.'
>
> Carry on Cleo, *movie*† (1964)

---

* There are of course memorable names in contemporary Egyptian history. A modern Egyptian father named his daughter 'Facebook' to celebrate the role Facebook played in the revolutionary Arab Spring of 2011. Her full name is Facebook Jamal Ibrahim.

† This is a classic film which (for reasons of professional jealousy) never won an Oscar; it was filmed on the set of *Cleopatra*, the movie starring Richard Burton and Elizabeth Taylor, which unaccountably won 4 (FOUR) Oscars. Infamy. The costume worn by Sidney James, as Mark Antony, in *Carry on Cleo* is the same one worn by Richard Burton as Mark Antony in the less-funny *Cleopatra*.

If you were Cleopatra you might be a little embarrassed by your parentage … and by your name. You'd be born the third child of the liaison between Ptolemy XII of Egypt and his half-sister. Your auntie was your mother and your uncle was your dad. Of course you are *not* embarrassed because this is an established custom among the Ptolemy rulers of Egypt. And you won't worry about the fact that your full name, Cleopatra Philopator, means 'lover of her father'. You're a real daddy's girl.

· 2 ·

'Never be haughty to the humble or humble to the haughty.'

> *Jefferson Davis (1808–89), President of the Confederate States of America during the Civil War*

George I was a German, parachuted onto the throne of the United Kingdom in 1714, who never troubled himself to learn English. Why bother? The Ptolemaic Dynasty was a family of Greek origin that ruled Egypt and, with Georgian arrogance, refused to speak Egyptian. As a result, Greek as well as Egyptian was used on official court records such as the Rosetta Stone.

The Rosetta Stone was found by one of Napoleon's invading soldiers 2,000 years after it was written. At last modern archaeologists, who could read Greek, could work out the meaning of those mysterious Egyptian squiggles – hieroglyphics. Thanks to the Ptolemies, the antique ptales could now be ptold.

In a break from tradition, Cleopatra *did* learn to speak Egyptian and presented herself as the reincarnation of an

Egyptian goddess, Isis. It must have worked because she ruled for 30 years' worth of dangerous days.

· 3 ·

> 'I like actors very much, but to marry one would be like marrying your brother. You look too much alike in the mirror.'
>
> *Marilyn Monroe (1926–62), American actress*

Cleopatra originally ruled jointly with her father, Ptolemy XII. Aged 18 when he died, she was joined on the throne by her 10 year-old brother, Ptolemy XIII. The boy-king's advisors ganged up to depose her, so she fled north to raise an army. Young Ptolemy welcomed the Roman General Julius Caesar to Egypt – I'd think that was as wise as welcoming a Nile crocodile to my hot tub.* Cleo now faced the might of Rome. Legend says she sneaked herself into Caesar's palace, rolled inside a carpet. When the carpet was unrolled she leapt out and did a little fraternising to win him over.

She gave birth to Caesar's child. Now that's what you call *really* fraternising with the enemy.† Their combined forces drove Ptolemy XIII to flight. He drowned in the Nile ... or was he pushed?‡

---

* I speak hypothetically. I don't have a hot tub. But if I did, I wouldn't invite a crocodile to share it. Though I guess that's equally hypothetical as I don't have any crocodiles in my Contacts' list.

† For historical balance it has to be said Caesar always denied fathering baby Caesarion, and there were no paternity tests to prove it one way or another.

‡ Ptolemy the *thirteenth* died on January the *thirteenth*. Not that any of us are Triskaidekaphobic ... but it makes you wonder.

Did you know ... in de Nile

The Nile was so revered as a giver of life it's easy to forget it also took many lives. One victim was Antinous, lover of Emperor Hadrian the wall-builder. When he drowned in the Nile in AD 130 Hadrian declared him a god and dedicated a new city, Antinopolis, to his name.* He was another who, like Caesarion, may have been pushed – a form of human sacrifice, some believe. The Nile had dangerous depths.

· 4 ·

> HORSA: 'Eh, Hengist, you will be thrown to the lions, in the arena. Don't worry. Head in the mouth, quick snap of the jaws and it'll all be over!'
>
> HENGIST: 'Yes, but how am I going to get his head into my mouth?'
>
> *Carry on Cleo*

The Egyptians hated to see Caesar come, see and conquer. Cleopatra wasn't their cup of Nile tea either. She gave her power some legitimacy by co-ruling with her next brother-in-line, Ptolemy XIV.

Cleo followed Caesar back to Rome, where he was famously stabbed to death by his friends in 44 BC.

Cleopatra wisely returned to Egypt. Husband-brother-co-ruler Ptolemy XIV died later in 44 BC. It seems likely Cleo had him poisoned so she could rule with baby Caesarion.

---

* It would be flattened by Pasha Mohammed Ali in the 1830s. Rest in pieces, Antinous.

· 5 ·

'Did my heart love till now? Forswear it, sight!
For I ne'er saw true beauty till this night.'

William Shakespeare: Romeo and Juliet

'I am glad it cannot happen twice, the fever of first
love. For it is a fever, and a burden, too, whatever the
poets may say.'

Daphne du Maurier (1907–89), English author: Rebecca

After Caesar's assassination, Rome was ruled by a triumvirate
and Mark Antony was the dominant force. He summoned
Cleopatra to Tarsus (in Turkey) to investigate her relations
with dead Julius Caesar. If life were like a Shakespeare
play, or a pop song, their eyes would meet as he kissed the
glittering rings on her hand and they'd fall instantly in love.

And sometimes it seems life *does* happen that way. It did
with this classic couple. *Romeo and Juliet* ended in tears
every bit as salty-sweet as Antony and Cleopatra's, but they
weren't to know that.

Antony followed Cleopatra to Egypt, where they famously
formed a drinking society called 'the Inimitable Livers'. The
cirrhotic livers may have been more apt.

Did you know ... love potions

The Egyptians had a love potion that would drive
women like Cleopatra wild with longing for a man.
You could try this at home but you may have trouble
collecting the ingredients:

🔲 Barley grains and apple pips

🔲 Your own blood and semen

🔲 The blood of a tick from a black dog✱

🔲 Dandruff from the scalp of a murder victim

Slip it into her drink and she will fall head over heels in love with you – if it doesn't poison her and make her fall head over heels into a coffin.

Antony and Cleopatra were together seven years – a thousand lifetimes compared to those mayflies Romeo and Juliet. They had twins – a boy and girl – then a son, but couldn't marry because Mark Antony had never divorced his third wife.

Some historians have said she was no great beauty. But, to impress him with her wealth, Cleo dropped a precious pearl in a flagon of wine and watched it dissolve. (We've all had bottles of wine like that from the supermarket bargain shelves. Never a waste of money as it can always double as paint-stripper or pearl-dissolving fluid.)

But Mark Antony was not secure in his Roman power base. He sensed there could be trouble ahead. After seven years it would be time to face the music and dance …

✱ A dog with ticks? Must be a watch-dog.

· 6 ·

'Till swollen with cunning, of a self-conceit,
His waxen wings did mount above his reach,
And melting heavens conspired his overthrow.'

Christopher Marlowe (1564–93),
English playwright: Doctor Faustus

Antony and Cleopatra's alliance was symbiotic. He got the money to tackle rival Roman Octavian and win back power, she saw the chance to reclaim Egypt's Eastern Empire (mainly Lebanon and Syria).

In 34 BC, Antony returned with Cleopatra to Alexandria with a triumphant flourish. Crowds swarmed to the city to catch a glimpse of the golden couple seated on golden thrones that were raised on silver platforms. Beside them sat their children.

But Antony was no Caesar on the battlefield or the seas. His navy met Octavian's fleet at Actium. Like the Armada 1,600 years later, the massive heavyweights (Egypt and Spain) were outmanoeuvred by the smaller ships (Rome and England). Antony's crews were weakened by a severe outbreak of malaria. He concentrated his numbers in heavy ships fitted with rams and burned the rest.

The manoeuvrable ships of Octavian didn't have Sir Francis Drake's cannon, but their catapulted stones would decapitate any of Antony's sailors who might be foolish enough to get their heads in the way. A defector took Antony's battle plans to Octavian and it was curtains for Cleo and co.

She saw the peril and signalled a retreat to the open sea to live and fight another day. Antony missed the signal and only saw the Queen of Egypt running off and deserting him. As firebrands landed amid his ships and caused panic, Antony abandoned his comrades and fled after Cleopatra.

Their futures did not look healthy.

· 7 ·

> 'Life is the farce which everyone has to perform.'
>
> *Arthur Rimbaud (1854–91), French poet*

What happened next was black comedy, tragedy, slapstick or Calamity Cleo, depending upon your view of life.

Cleo fled to Egypt and locked herself in her treasury to avoid the wrath of Antony, who blamed her for their defeat. He struggled to hold back Octavian's invasion then ...

◻ Antony heard a rumour that Cleopatra was dead.

◻ He fell on his sword ... but didn't do a very good job.*

◻ As he lingered, he heard the rumours of Cleo's death were false. He wanted to live.

◻ He died.

Some stories say he was carried to Cleopatra's retreat and died in her bed. Sweet.

---

* He guessed he'd botch the job so he asked his servant Eros to kill him. Eros said, 'I'd rather kill myself,' and proceeded to do so. Antony was inspired by the servant's example and stabbed himself ... and botched it just as he'd known he would. Sometimes you just can't get the servants.

· 8 ·

> 'Always carry a flagon of whiskey in case of snakebite
> … and furthermore always carry a small snake.'
>
> W. C. Fields

The death of Cleopatra is probably not as spectacular as the legend of the asp to the bosom everyone remembers.

The queen tried to negotiate with Octavian. The deal she offered was that she would renounce the throne if he would let her children rule in her place. As he kept her talking at the locked door of her retreat, his officers sneaked up to the window on a ladder to apprehend her. When she saw them she took a dagger and tried to kill herself. Like lover Antony before her, she missed. (No wonder they lost the battle of Actium when they were such rotten shots.)

She was freed to arrange Antony's funeral then sank into a depression. She knew her fate was to be paraded through the streets of Rome like a trophy of war. She would rather die. But how to do it when she was closely guarded?

There are two versions of what happened next …

(i) Cleopatra had a basket of figs delivered and it contained a snake. She wrote to Octavian to say, 'Let me be buried with Marc Antony,' before pressing the snake to her much-admired bosom, suffering the snakebite and dying. Her maids died too. That's the version Shakespeare adapted. (We don't know what happened to the asp.)

OR …

(ii) Octavian's guards killed her. A credible story. After all, the asp story is full of holes. Egyptians didn't commit suicide because they'd never get into the afterlife. And asp bites are slow to work – the guards could have saved her. Octavian was determined to exterminate the royal line and had her son killed. Why would he not have Cleopatra killed ... then bump off the maids so they couldn't sell their story to the Daily Egyptian Mail?

Whatever the tragic truth, the two were buried together, as they had wished, and Egypt became a province of the Roman Empire. The Roman province of Aegyptus.

And that was pretty much the end of the history of Ancient Egypt.

Did you know ... Cleopatra

Cleo is a pharaoh as much exploited for profit as Tutankhamun. She may not have been amused by the 20th-century US advert in which a model which claimed:

'I dreamt I was Cleopatra sailing down the Nile in my Maidenform bra.'

We have to ask, 'Why was Cleopatra sailing down the Nile in a bra?' Surely she should be in a barge?

AWFUL ARCHAEOLOGISTS

'An archaeologist is the best husband a woman can have.
The older she gets the more interested he is in her.'
Agatha Christie (1890–1976), English crime writer

'When digging ceases to be a great game and becomes,
as in Egypt, merely business, it will be a bad thing.'
Sir Charles Leonard Woolley (1880–1960), British archaeologist

Little did the pharaohs realise that their corpses would become big business in the grubbing world of their distant futures.

Of all the grave-robbers the 19th-century relic hunters were the most prolific. As the interest in Egyptian history grew, so did the profits. The word 'scruples' appeared to have been deleted from the dictionary of the diggers and despoilers.

If the archaeologist-robbers were alive now, they would point to our museums and say, 'You owe all these ancient treasures to us. We rescued them for you. And if we made a fortune or achieved fame … or both … then who are you to begrudge it?'

These colourful corpse- and coffin-cracking filchers led interesting lives. Some were larger than life.

— HENRY SALT (1780–1827) —

English artist, collector, diplomat, and Egyptologist

> 'The "polymath" had already died out by the close of the eighteenth century, and in the following century intensive education replaced extensive, so that by the end of it the specialist had evolved.'
>
> *Dietrich Bonhoeffer (1906–45), German pastor**

Like so many early Egyptologists, Salt came from a varied background that made him unqualified to excavate. He learned 'on the job'. He trained as a painter who pottered round the East to paint. Because he became familiar with Egypt he was appointed British Consul-General in Cairo. That's the way it worked.

That position gave him a platform to loot the treasures of Ancient Egypt … not for Britain but for the highest bidder. Once he lost his ambassadorial job he was free to assemble antiquities. He found his French and Italian rivals were making it a cut-throat business. As Salt didn't say …

---

* Bonhoeffer was a leader of resistance to the Nazi dictatorship, and involved with the plot to assassinate Adolf Hitler. He was eventually arrested in April 1943 by the Gestapo and imprisoned for one and a half years. After a very brief, biased trial, he was executed by hanging on 9 April 1945, just two weeks before Allied forces liberated the camp.

> 'Italians cannot beat us, but we can certainly lose
> against them.'
> *Johan Cruyff (1947–), Dutch footballer*

Salt gathered his own team of relentless thugs. By 1827 he had sold his collection to the British Museum for £2,000 and started a new one. When it reached over 4,000 objects he put it up for auction again. The British Museum couldn't afford it so it was sold to the Louvre in Paris for £10,000. Business was booming.

His third collection sold to the British Museum in 1835, but Salt didn't earn a penny. He had died eight years earlier. Careless.

Salt had set a precedent – Egyptian loot was liquid gold and the museums were paying handsomely for someone else's treasures.

— BERNARDINO DROVETTI (1776–1852) —

> 'A small body of determined spirits fired by an
> unquenchable faith in their mission can alter the
> course of history.'
> *Mahatma Gandhi*

But not always for the better, Mr Gandhi. If Salt was a determined collector of antiquities and cash then Drovetti was his ruthless rival. The French ambassador to Egypt, Drovetti hindered Salt as much as he could in a dog-eat-dog battle.

His methods were breathtakingly brutal. If he found a tomb with 20 alabaster vases then he deemed them too common – a drug on the market. So he smashed half of them and made the remainder rarer ... and more valuable.

He was known to break off the tip of an obelisk to make it easier to transport.

Nowadays he'd be pilloried for cultural vandalism. In his native Italy he had statues raised to him.

Salt and Drovetti both gave money to local chiefs who then saw to it that other collectors were either warned off or not supplied with labour.

When it came to the obelisks in Philae, Salt was commissioned to send one of the six-ton monsters to a private collector in England, William Bankes. Salt was lucky enough to have the giant Italian adventurer Giovanni Belzoni as his agent – the strongman of Egyptology.

Drovetti claimed that the objects belonged to him, but appeared to concede ownership to Bankes. Belzoni was convinced that Drovetti had been defeated by the problems of transporting the obelisk. Drovetti wasn't so easily deterred. He simply had a better plan.

Belzoni had the obelisk levered and pushed on rollers to a solid wooden pier for shipping down the Nile. The Italian had to use all his ingenuity and strength to make the short trip to the waiting ship. He later admitted it was almost a disaster …

> 'But, alas, when the obelisk came gradually from the sloping bank and all its weight rested on it, the pier, the obelisk and some of the men, took a slow movement, and majestically descended into the river.'
>
> *Giovanni Battista Belzoni (1778–1823), Italian explorer*

Belzoni and his men hauled it out of the mud and got it loaded onto a boat for its journey to Cairo.

The hard work was over … and Drovetti had let Belzoni do it all. Then the French ambassador struck. Drovetti's men intercepted Belzoni on his way to Aswan. It was the sort of ambush that Jesse James, Ned Kelly, Butch Cassidy or Dick Turpin would have been proud to own. It was only after a long struggle, which ended in gunfire, that the hijackers were driven off.

The obelisk was shipped to England in May 1821 and erected in Bankes' garden in 1827. It is there, on the south coast of England to this day. It is as at home there as a camel in Lapland.

It had almost been stolen en route. A Bankes robbery, in fact.

King Charles Felix of Sardinia acquired much of the Drovetti collection in 1824. The Frenchman had asset-stripped Egyptian history of 5,268 pieces, including 100 statues, 170 papyri, stelae and mummies.

Did you know ... Cleopatra's Needle

The obelisk that stands on the banks of the River Thames is actually Thutmose III's Needle – it was erected in Egypt in 1450 BC, over a thousand years before Cleopatra was born.

In 1877 the obelisk was loaded into a sealed tube of steel and floated into the Mediterranean. It had its own cabin, crew and mast, but no power. It would be towed to London by a grain-carrier ship.

If the captains of the two vessels wanted to communicate they used a megaphone in good weather and a blackboard in bad. It was as dangerous a few weeks as the seas have ever seen.

The steel tube rolled badly in a storm off the coast of France. A boat sent out to stabilise it sank and six seamen died. The curse of Thutmose?

Another British ship salvaged the steel tube and it finally arrived in England. The dead seamen are remembered on a plaque.

— GASTON MASPERO (1846–1916) —

> 'When thieves fall out, honest men come by their own.'
>
> *English proverb*

Not all the Europeans were thieves and profiteers. In 1880 Gaston Maspero headed a French expedition to Egypt as director-general of excavations.

One of his primary tasks was to curb the rampant illegal export of Egyptian antiquities. Everyone was at it – not just the occasional acquisitive tourist or collector. The biggest dealers were the agents who plundered the ancient sites on behalf of the major European and American museums.

A cache of 36 mummies had been hidden by ancient priests at Deir el-Bahari. They may have been found as early as 1860 by the three Abd al-Rassul brothers who had 20 profitable years letting the ancient treasures seep onto the market. But when Maspero arrived, he set off to investigate.

Maspero arrested the brothers from the notorious treasure-hunting village of Qurna. The locals swore to the honesty of the family. Gaston was unimpressed. Naturally the family had not stayed in business for 20 years by betraying their secrets, and they weren't going to give anything away to some French Egyptologist. Gaston called in the local authorities, who tortured the brothers.

None of them cracked. However Mohammed el-Rassul, the eldest brother, was so furious with his family for letting him suffer he demanded 50 per cent of future profits. They refused and argued bitterly.

Mohammed then turned informer, and went to the authorities to divulge the location of the hidden tomb. He told a remarkable story that would make a good plot for an Indiana Jones movie. He said that one day, 20 years before, a goat belonging to brother Ahmed had strayed from its herd on the cliffs in the bay of Deir el-Bahari. When Ahmed followed the bleating of his animal, he found that it had fallen down one of the vertical tomb-shafts that honeycombed the cliffs.

Ahmed cursed the goat, but climbed down after it and found himself in a poky corridor, cluttered with dark shapes. The goat-herd lit a candle and saw that the shapes were a collection of dusty wooden coffins heaped one upon another.

But as the bard had said …

> 'All that glisters is not gold;
> Often have you heard that told.'*
>
> *William Shakespeare:* Merchant of Venice

And all that's dusty is not dross. Ahmed could see the occasional 'uraeus' carving, the royal cobra, and several cartouches inscribed on the coffin lids. He soon realised that this was a royal find, an Aladdin's cave of treasure.

The three brothers slowly fed their finds onto the collectors' market and lived comfortably for 20 years. They

---

* The Bard had borrowed that from Chaucer's *Canterbury Tales* perhaps. Chaucer wrote, 'All thing which that shineth as the gold / Ne is no gold, as I have heard it told.'

never revealed the goose that was laying the glistering eggs until Mohammed was tortured.

Family traitor Mohammed took the officials to Deir el-Bahari where he showed them the actual tomb chamber, which contained coffins of some of Ancient Egypt's greatest kings of the New Kingdom. Much had disappeared and the gold sarcophagi had been melted down. The mummies had been stripped to recover the bandaged jewels, then re-wrapped.

Gaston Maspero had returned to France by this time, so Emile Brugsch, an assistant, was called in to investigate the find and remove most of the objects to the national museum. As they headed down the Nile to Cairo, the local people lined the banks and wailed and ground dust into their heads, just as Ancient Egyptian mourners had done thousands of years before – a sign of grief for what they'd lost.

Thieves tried to attack and rob the convoy, but guards fought them off. They reached the safety of Cairo museum.

And what happened to traitor-brother Mohammed? He was given a £500 reward ... and placed in charge of the subsequent excavations. Who better?

In 1914 Gaston Maspero introduced Lord Carnarvon to archaeologist Howard Carter – the twosome who discovered the tomb of Tutankhamun in 1922. But Maspero had died in 1916 so never got to see the crowning glory of his efforts.

— GIOVANNI BATTISTA BELZONI —
(1778–1823)

> 'Belzoni was one of the most remarkable men in the
> entire history of Archaeology.'
>
> *Howard Carter (1873–1939), archaeologist*

'The Great Belzoni' was just 45 when he died but crammed
a lot into his life and left his footprints on the sands of time.
At 6 foot 7 inches tall, they would have been deep footprints.
Briefly…

👁 Belzoni was Italian by birth, one of 13 children. His plans
to become a monk were disrupted when Napoleon's
French army occupied Rome. He trained briefly as a
hydraulic engineer. That would be useful – eventually.

👁 He moved to Holland to become a barber like his
father. He fled to England to avoid jail and married
the formidable Sarah Bane. They performed at fairs
and on the streets of London as a strongman and a
strongwoman act under the name 'The Great Belzoni'.
This career lasted for ten years.

👁 They left the circus in 1812, and went to Malta, where
he met an officer of Mohammed Ali Pasha, who
invited him to Egypt.* Belzoni wanted to show Pasha

---

* Mohammed Ali Pasha (1769–1845) was an interesting character in his
own right. He was an Albanian commander in the Ottoman army. He
became self-declared Khedive of Egypt and Sudan with the Ottoman's
temporary approval. He is credited as the founder of modern Egypt
because of the major reforms he instigated in military, economic and
cultural spheres. He didn't seem too bothered about saving the national
treasures that the rich Victorian museums were removing wholesale.

a hydraulic machine of his own invention for raising the waters of the Nile River. The machine worked but Pasha wasn't enthused and abandoned the project.

In Egypt, Belzoni met and joined British Consul-General Henry Salt, who worked on transporting the Egyptian treasures to the British Museum. For several years, Belzoni moved thousands of artefacts. When his 'hydraulics' failed, he employed brute force.

Being untrained in archaeological methods, Belzoni caused damage to various sites he explored. In order to remove a sarcophagus in the Valley of the Kings, he made a hole in the decorated, ancient wall and destroyed a large piece of original artwork. Pragmatist or plunderer? Profiteer or pioneer?

He was certainly cynical about depriving Egyptians of their heritage. Before he left Egypt, Belzoni was asked, 'Are you so short of stones in Europe that you have to come here to take ours?' 'No,' he replied. 'But we prefer the Egyptian sort.'

By 1820 Belzoni had enough treasure to hold several exhibitions in London and Paris. The interest in the ancient world was being awakened. But the profits were disappointing. The giant needed a new gigantic challenge.

In 1823 Belzoni set off to explore the course of the Niger River and find the mythical city of Timbuktu. He went by the Guinea coastal route and reached Benin, but contracted dysentery. He died there and was buried under an arasma tree in Gwato.

Belzoni, a circus giant with enormous energy who filled the British Museum with riches. His successors were reluctant to call him a robber. Howard Carter praised him …

> 'This was the first occasion on which excavations on a large scale had ever been made in the Valley of the Kings, and we must give Belzoni full credit for the manner in which they were carried out.'

… but there was a qualification …

> 'There are episodes which give the modern excavator rather a shock, as, for example, when he describes his method of dealing with sealed doorways – by means of a battering ram – but on the whole the work was extraordinarily good.'

How polite and understated is that? 'Rather a shock'? It was a jaw-dropping, outrageous and appalling piece of vandalism.

But even his dodgy dealings are overshadowed by the British Museum's acquisition of 'Ginger' …

⁓ DEATH ON THE NILE ⁓

> 'Forensic scientists have moved closer to solving a 5,500-year-old cold case crime after new technology allowed them to study fatal wounds on the body of a famous mummy.'*
>
> *Hannah Furness, Daily Telegraph, 16 November 2012*

---

* Bit of dramatic licence there. 'Solving' the crime generally means identifying the culprit. The guilty party has been dead for 5,500 years or 100 years and is not named. But it makes for a catchy intro to an article.

The oldest mummy on display to the world is thought to be 'Ginger' – a relic of the days before the pharaohs ruled. He wasn't a neatly dried and bandaged boy but a sun-dried mummy. He was buried at Gebelein near Luxor about 3200 BC, just left in a shallow grave in the sand. His dead body was perfectly dried and preserved by the action of hot dry sand. The sand absorbed the moisture from the body as well as any ancient embalmer's natron salt.

But the facts and fictions surrounding this sun-shrivelled Egyptian may be a murder story as old as time … or as recent as a Jack-the-Ripper victim.

One version of the finding says three well-preserved bodies were excavated in 1896 by Wallis Budge, the British Museum Keeper for Egyptology. Since 1901 the first of the excavated bodies has remained on display in the British Museum. He was nicknamed 'Ginger' due to his red hair.*

But there is another tale far more suited to a study of dangerous days in Egypt. The story goes that in 1896 the British Museum let it be known that it badly wanted an ancient mummy to exhibit. An Egyptian dealer just happened to have exactly what the BM was looking for. A happy happenstance? Yes, but the vendor was a rather notorious Egyptian antiques dealer. And anything he had to offer had to be viewed with suspicion.

––––––––

* It is no longer politically correct to label him Ginger so the nickname has been quietly changed to 'Gebelein predynastic mummy'. Redheads of the world unite, Gingerism is dead. When he was temporarily removed for restoration in 1897 he was replaced with a female mummy. She had long brown hair but, in his honour, she was nicknamed Gingerella. How times change. The BM aren't rejecting Gingerism – they are showing respect by ethical treatment of human remains. So Ginger Rogers probably needs to be renamed 'Gebelein predynastic mummy formerly dance partner to Fred Astaire … Rogers'.

At the same time, one of that dodgy dealer's relations disappeared mysteriously, believed murdered. The young missing person was of the same size and features as Ginger. Surely the dealer couldn't have passed off his brother as a mummified ancient? It would be two birds with one stone – cover up the crime *and* make a profit. Unlikely, you would think. The BM would never buy a murder victim. Never.

Except …

◻ Budge didn't exactly 'discover' the sun-dried corpses. Budge was approached by a resident of Gebelein who claimed to have found more mummies. Budge was led to Ginger's grave. A fraud could have been perpetrated.

◻ In November 2012 it was revealed that Ginger … sorry, 'The Gebelein predynastic mummy …. formerly known as Ginger' – had been murdered. A CAT scan showed he had been aged about 18 to 20 at the time of his death and had been well muscled. Under his left shoulder blade there was a puncture wound to the body. The murder weapon had shattered the rib beneath it and penetrated the lung. It was the sort of injury that might be caused by a copper blade or flint knife at least 12 cm in length. There were no defence wounds on the hands or arms – Gebelein predynastic etc. had been taken by surprise, and probably not in battle.

So you decide. Ancient crime? Or a Victorian case for Sherlock Holmes?

— WALLIS BUDGE (1857–1934) —
Egyptologist

> 'Reason, Observation and Experience — the Holy
> Trinity of Science — have taught us that happiness is
> the only good; that the time to be happy is now, and
> the way to be happy is to make others so. If the
> existence of a power superior to nature shall be
> demonstrated, there will then be time enough to
> kneel. Until then, let us stand erect.'
>
> *Robert G. Ingersoll (1833–99), US lawyer and agnostic*

In 1896 there was dirty work afoot in the world of antiquities. Precious ancient writings had been found in Iraq and the tablets were guarded by agents of the British Museum. Yet several of the 'guarded' tablets began appearing in the shop-windows of London antiquities' dealers. The BM had to buy their own artefacts back at market rates. 'That is so not fair,' the principal librarian whined. 'No one should be pillaging those excavations … except us, of course.'

The word went out, 'Send our up-and-coming Egyptologist, young Wallis Budge, to investigate.' While he was there, they decided, he could set up links with dealers in Iran – 'We want first refusal on your best finds,' was the message.*

Budge performed well in Iran then moved on to Egypt to do the same. He sent back shiploads of tablets and papyri and manuscripts. At a time when the world's museums were scrapping to plunder the past, Budge made sure the Brits had the best.

---

* A cunning plan that meant the British Museum didn't have to invest any money themselves in the excavations.

By 1900 an archaeologist was praising burglar Budge as a true hero ...

> 'What a revolution you have effected in the Museum! It is now a veritable history of civilisation in a series of object lessons.'
>
> *Archibald Sayce (1846–1933), Assyriologist*

The museum marauders were unscrupulous in their methods. When Egypt tried to stem the bleeding of its past, the European museum officials and their local agents simply smuggled antiquities in diplomatic pouches, or bribed customs officials and employees of the Egyptian Service of Antiquities – the guardians of Egypt's treasures.

Mild mannered Budge had his enemies in Egypt. In 1893 he was sued in the high court by an Egyptian called Hormuzd Rassam. Budge had written that Rassam was a 'smuggler' who had been sending only 'rubbish' to the British Museum. Budge apologised to Rassam for his offensive comments and the Museum avoided damaging libel costs – but as Budge's bosses were paying well for antiquities he was rather shameless in criticising the methods of the local suppliers. Calling Rassam a smuggler? Pot, kettle, black.

Budge's views on Egypt's religion were a little skewed by his own interest in the paranormal. He was a believer in spirits and hauntings. His best friends were members of the 'Ghost Club' – a London group who studied religions and the spirit world. He liked to tell his own twisted tales of hauntings and eerie experiences.* Was he unscientific then?

---

* Many people to this day are devotees of Budge's spooky works, especially his translation of the Egyptian Book of the Dead.

> 'Now about those ghosts. I'm sure they're here and I'm
> not half so alarmed at meeting up with any of them
> as I am at having to meet the live nuts I have to see
> every day.'
>
> *Elizabeth 'Bess' Truman (1885–1982), First Lady of the United States*

Wallis's reputation as an Egyptologist has faded. His critics
say he wrote 'facts' that were in fact merely 'opinions'.

Odd. I thought all historians did that.

— A BURNING ISSUE —

One of Wallis Budge's friends was the adventure writer
Sir Henry Rider Haggard. He seems to have used Budge's
knowledge of Egypt as the basis for his fiction.

In the Rider Haggard novel *She*, the bitumen-soaked
mummy limbs made flaming torches for the natives. Oh,
how he must have enjoyed writing that Gothic horror sketch.

> '"Great heaven!" he said. "They are corpses on fire!"
>
> I stared and stared again – he was perfectly right
> – the torches that were to light our entertainment
> were human mummies from the caves!
>
> Heavens! How they roared and flared! No tar
> barrel could have burnt as those mummies did. Nor
> was this all. Suddenly I saw one great fellow seize a
> flaming human arm that had fallen from its parent
> frame, and rush off into the darkness.
>
> Presently he stopped, and a tall streak of fire shot
> up into the air, illumining the gloom, and also the
> lamp from which it sprang. That lamp was the

mummy of a woman tied to a stout stake let into the
rock, and he had fired her hair. At last we were
surrounded on all three sides by a great ring of bodies
flaring furiously, so inflammable that the flames
would literally spout out of the ears and mouth in
tongues of fire a foot or more in length.'

Sir Henry Rider Haggard (1856–1925), English author: She

But corpses as fuel? That was widely believed a hundred years
ago. There's a tasteless story, apocryphal, about the burning
of mummies as fuel in Victorian steam locomotives in Egypt.

'I shall not speak of the Egyptian railway, for it is like
any other railway – I shall only say that the fuel they
use for the locomotive is composed of mummies
three thousand years old, purchased by the ton or by
the graveyard for that purpose. Sometimes one hears
the profane engineer call out pettishly, "Damn these
commoners, they don't burn worth a cent – toss me
up a King."'

Mark Twain: Innocents Abroad

Mark Twain popularised the tale of mummy-powered steam
trains, but there's no evidence it was true. His fiction persists
as an urban myth that many still believe.

However, what *is* certain is that mummies supplied the
fuel for household fires in Thebes through the 1800s and for
Bedouin campfires.*

---

* We revere mummies in glass cases in museums these days and are
shocked by the vandalism of ancient mummies destroyed for profit. But
for every mummy preserved there were a hundred or more obliterated
when modern Egypt flooded the Nile Valley to construct the Aswan Dam
in the 1960s.

— THE MUMMY MISERY —

'I think if you're an entrepreneur, you've got to dream big and then dream bigger.'

Howard D. Schultz (1953—), American businessman

In the Victorian age Americans got it into their heads that they believed that mummies had healing powers. They ground up the mummies into powder and used it as medicine. But other desiccated and desecrated corpses were treated with less respect. Or were they?

It's a mysterious tale. In the USA in the 1850s there was a shortage of paper. Newspapers were expanding their circulation and someone very clever calculated the industry needed almost half a billion pounds of rags, each year, to be pulped and manufactured into paper.

Where would they find rags? Wrapped around mummies, perhaps? After all, Egypt had been wrapping corpses for 3,000 years, so there was a fair rag-and-bone-yard stock to mine.

The English Egyptologist Dr Pettigrew had taken his unwrapping display to the US and there were mummies displayed in travelling shows ... alongside the bearded ladies and Feejee mermaids, Tom Thumb and the Siamese twins, Chang and Eng. Such indignity. What ignominy. How mortifying ... really mortifying. The downside of having your body preserved for eternity.

Somewhere some entrepreneur mentally deconstructed the displays and saw not kings and corpses but *bandages*. Linen. Precious paper-making material. Cash for corpses. Paper money. It was Dr Isaiah Deck (a New Yorker, though English by birth) who was that entrepreneur. He noted that a princess from Dr Pettigrew's collection was wrapped in 40 layers, requiring 42 yards of fine linen.

An 1847 trip to Egypt revealed a fortune in pharaohs' and friends' mummies.* Deck calculated there must be half a billion mummies in Egypt. Add in mummified cats, bulls and crocodiles, and the number increases again.† There was enough to keep the US in paper for 14 years, his sums said. The mummies of the poor were conveniently collected into pits; time and erosion had almost uncovered them. Opencast mummy mining.

> 'It is by no means rare to find above thirty pounds' weight of linen wrappings on mummies.'
>
> *Dr Isaiah Deck, US geologist*

In 1855 Deck wrote that mummy cloth could be shipped to the US for 3 cents a pound – half the price of existing raw rag material. By 1863 the American Civil War drove up demand still further, so several shiploads of mummies were imported to a Maine paper-mill. The workers who converted the bandages to paper began to fall ill and die from cholera. The mummies were blamed.

Cholera is a bacterium and active disease cells were unlikely to have survived for centuries in the wrappings.

The truth is it was more likely to be from

a) the contaminated water the workers were obliged to drink; OR

---

* Just a few years later, in 1854, an Englishman called Hill found a couple of new paper-making materials – radishes and horse manure. The latter is, you'll agree, a very appropriate raw material for making some books.
† Deck explained that the burned bones of the sacred bulls of Dahshur were already being used in the sugar-refining processes of Lower Egypt. I'd steer clear. Bull … steer … never mind.

b) The infection came from modern rags imported from
France and Italy.

The story grew that cholera outbreaks were being spread by
shopkeepers wrapping meat in brown mummy paper. It was
a revenge of the Ancient Dead.

But the entire story is unproven. There is no evidence that
Deck's idea was ever adopted or that mummies were pulped
for paper.

There is even a suspicion that Deck was a joker – he made
an outrageous suggestion with a straight face and was taken
seriously by the humourless people of this world.

Yet again, placing the blame on a mummy 'curse' turns out
to be unfounded.

⟶ PROS AND CON ARTISTS ⟵

> 'Pettigrew was one day unrolling a mummy in
> his house in Savile Row before some friends, and
> was just remarking that he had come across some
> hieroglyphics which would give him the name of
> the mummy, when a maidservant came in and
> overheard the remark. She went back to the kitchen
> and told the others that the master had just found
> out the name of the mummy and that it was
> "Harry Griffiths" (Hieroglyphics).'
>
> *Anecdote told by Pettigrew's grandson*

As the fashion for studying mummies flourished in the
Victorian age there was always someone prepared to make a
dodgy dollar or a suspect senyu from the gullible.

Pettigrew himself came across an Egyptian who spent his days inside a pyramid manufacturing mummies for sale to museums and collectors. He was only the tip of the pyramid.

From 1837 onwards many mummies and their coffins were manufactured and 'distressed' like dodgy antiques. Anyone buying from a Cairo back-street dealer was liable to be conned. When they were unwrapped, the mummies turned out to comprise …

- Modern paper and cotton balls
- Ibis bones
- Wood, wire and clay constructions
- Animal teeth

As recently as 2001 the mummified body of the daughter of Persian King Xerxes (519–465 BC) was offered for sale in Pakistan. Suspicious buyers had it tested and it proved to be not only a recent corpse but one that looked suspiciously like a murder victim.

— SIR FLINDERS PETRIE (1853–1942) —

Brace yourself for this quote. Albert Einstein was a genius. So some of his statements may make the brain cell of an ordinary human ache.*

---

* Who am I calling 'ordinary', you snap and snarl. Me, dear reader, me.

> 'Science is the century-old endeavour to bring together
> by means of systematic thought the perceptible
> phenomena of this world into as thoroughgoing an
> association as possible. To put it boldly, it is the attempt
> at the posterior reconstruction of existence by the
> process of conceptualisation.'
>
> *Albert Einstein*

Science takes chaos and creates order ... I think.

The early Egyptologists were trophy-hunters, the curious, the greedy, the adventurers and the dreamers. What Egyptology needed was someone with a system and a wish to conserve.

That man was Flinders Petrie and he didn't arrive on the scene a moment too soon. In fact, given the depredations of men like destroyer-Drovetti and battering-ram-Belzoni, some of the past was already in the landfill site of history.

Young Flinders, home-educated, was only eight when the idea of a systematic dig took hold. Friends visiting the Petrie family were describing the unearthing of the Brading Roman villa on the Isle of Wight. The boy was appalled to hear of the rough digging techniques, and claimed the earth should be pared away, inch by inch.

> 'All that I have done since was there to begin with. I
> was already in archaeology by nature.'
>
> *Sir Flinders Petrie's autobiography:* Seventy Years*

The prodigy's perfect principle pervades digs to this day.

---

* Albert Einstein's brain was removed and pickled for scientific study when he died in 1955. Flinders Petrie had gone one better and willed his head to science when he died in 1942. It would be nice to think the two brains could get together some time. A marvellous meeting of marinated minds.

Did you know ... family affairs

Flinders Petrie made an astonishing discovery from
the tombs of the ordinary Ancient Egyptians who
had been mummified. From the inscriptions on the
mummies he found that the dead and embalmed
relatives were kept with their living families for
generations before being buried.*

He began cutting his teeth (as it were) on British sites and
by the age of 19 had produced the most accurate survey of
Stonehenge to date. He graduated to the pyramids in 1880.
If he'd been shocked by the Isle of Wight Roman dig he was
mortified by the mistreatment of old Egypt's treasures.

> 'Egypt was a house on fire, so rapid was the
> destruction. My duty was that of a salvage man,
> to get all I could as quickly as possible and then,
> when I was 60, I would sit and write it all.'

Petrie was financially backed by the Egypt Exploration
Society, so wasn't under pressure to sell to fund the digs.
He began sending his finds to the Egyptian 'Department
Of Antiquities' for preservation. They were left in the care
of Gaston Maspero. Imagine Petrie's disappointment when
he discovered some of his great finds – 60 pharaoh portraits
– were left in a back yard of the museum to rot. Flinders
fumed. Maspero put the best 12 on display and sent the other
48 to Petrie to be displayed in London.

The road to conservation was an uphill one.

---

* In the days before television I guess a mummified granddad in the
corner could make a bit of a conversation piece at dinner parties?

Did you know ... Flash Flinders

Sir Flinders Petrie was irritated by women tourists who came to pore over his digs and ask questions. He took to wearing pink tights. When he emerged from a tomb he would appear to be naked from the waist down. The prim Victorian ladies would flee.

⌐ AMELIA EDWARDS (1831–92) ⌐

'What is feminism? Simply the belief that women should be as free as men ... however nuts, dim, deluded, badly dressed, fat, receding, lazy and smug they might be.'

Caitlin Moran (1975—), British broadcaster and journalist

Women Egyptologists were as rare as women pharaohs. Some adopted Egypt as a hobby or collected what the blokes were digging up. Some, like Amelia Edwards, dipped deeply into their purses and backed archaeological expeditions.

Amelia was a Victorian novelist who wrote some racy stuff, like *Barbara's History* (about bigamy) and the ever-popular ghost story *The Phantom Coach*. Her coach story still appears in anthologies today, even though its purple prose seems a little dated. A grouse-shooter is lost on the moors in a snow-storm and hitches a ride in a coach – his fellow passengers are the living dead ...

> 'A shriek of terror, a wild unintelligible cry for help
> and mercy, burst from my lips as I flung myself
> against the door, and strove in vain to open it.'*

This passionate supporter of women's suffrage never married but travelled for much of her life with a female companion. Having made her fortune she decided to take a trip to Egypt and began a love affair with the place and its history. If her novels had been a success then the journal of her travel became a best-selling phenomenon. The over-the-top style echoes her novelist roots ...

> 'Happy are the Nile travellers who start thus with a
> fair breeze on a brilliant afternoon. The good boat
> cleaves her way swiftly and steadily. Water-side
> palaces and gardens glide by, and are left behind.'
>
> *Amelia Edwards:* A Thousand Miles up the Nile

Melodramatic prose. But her concern for conservation gave the Victorian pillagers pause for thought ...

> 'Every day, more inscriptions are mutilated –
> more paintings and sculptures are defaced. When
> science leads the way, is it wonderful that ignorance
> should follow?'

She befriended archaeologists like Flinders Petrie and Gaston Maspero. In 1882 Amelia co-founded the Egypt Exploration Fund to back further digs. She abandoned her fiction-writing to concentrate on Egyptology, embarking on an ambitious lecture tour in America. In her absence, the fund she had

---

* Who hasn't felt that way? Trapped in a car with a bad driver?

founded began to marginalise her. Her greatest fault was to be a woman in a male-dominated world of Victorian archaeology.

The intrepid traveller had braved flies, mud, cold, heat, poor roads and hostile natives. Her ending wasn't as glamorous as an Egyptian queen. First her woman companion of 30 years died and left the writer bereft. Months later Amelia died of flu in Weston-Super-Mare.

She was buried with an Egyptian obelisk as a gravestone.

— HOWARD CARTER (1874–1939) —

> 'There is only one moment in time when it is necessary to awaken. That moment is now.'
>
> *Buddha (563–483 BC), Indian teacher*

One moment in time can define a person for life. The moment Neil Armstrong stepped onto the Moon – the world remembered him. The moment Archduke Ferdinand of Austria took a bullet in the neck or King Harold of England took an arrow in the eye – the world remembered them. It's as if the rest of their lives were defined by those few ticks of time.

So it was with Howard Carter, the English archaeologist. When he shone a light into the tomb of Tutankhamun and said he saw 'Wonderful things'. The world remembers him for that, even though there were many years of struggle that led him to that moment.

> 'Howard Carter can rightly be called an unsung hero of Egyptology, a man forever outshone by his discovery.'*
>
> *Archaeological Institute of America report*

---

* He was hardly 'unsung' … but we know what the writer means.

There were years of study to arrive at his magical moment. He initially trained as an artist – a skill that would prove useful for an archaeologist. In 1891 he went to Egypt and at the age of just 17 he devised a way of recording tomb inscriptions. He was so devoted to his work he slept with the bats in the tombs at night.

He studied for a year under Flinders Petrie – who privately believed young Howard would never make a top excavator. The young man proved his teacher wrong and made some important finds.

But Carter's personality was too formidable for his own good at times and he lived his own dangerous days. On more than one occasion he tracked and confronted tomb-robbers.

In 1902 Carter was accused by a disgruntled antiquities dealer at Luxor of 'unprofessional dealings'. Carter was said to have used his position to sell antiquities before they were recorded. The dealer also charged Carter with illegally abetting Wallis Budge to smuggle Egyptian antiquities for the British Museum collection without a licence.

Carter's boss, Gaston Maspero, backed Carter and he dodged the charges. But Maspero moved Carter away from Upper Egypt. He also described him as 'obstinate' – a character flaw that almost ruined his reputation. Carter's career all but imploded in 1904 when he was 30. He became entangled in* … the Saqqara Affair.

Carter had been specialising in the Valley of the Kings for over a decade when Gaston Maspero transferred him to work in Lower Egypt. Carter appeared happy with the move.

---

* Pause for roll of drums and dramatic music here. Can you hear them? Good. Now read on.

'I am now down in Cairo for good. It's a nice change though perhaps not so interesting. But after 11 years in Thebes one can get a little tired and slack.'

Howard Carter: letter to Lord Amherst, 1904

If he'd had an efficient crystal ball, Carter's 'for good' would have become 'for a few weeks'. It was all down to that stubborn streak and to the curse of the tourist. Flinders Petrie described ... the Saqqara Affair. He wrote it in his memoirs and remembered some of the facts correctly...

'One Sunday some drunken Frenchmen tried to force their way into the archaeologists' huts and were stoutly resisted by the cook boy. They went on to the official house and began to smash furniture and fight the native guards. Carter, the inspector, was fetched and he very rightly allowed the guards to defend themselves until the police came.

The French Consul demanded an apology from Carter for allowing native guards to resist French citizens. Carter refused to apologise for doing his duty. For this he was, on demand of the French, dismissed from the service. This was perhaps the dirtiest act of subservience to French arrogance.'*

But Petrie misremembered much of the ... Saqqara Affair. Carter's own account said ...

---

* You get the feeling Flinders Petrie did not love the French, whose Gaston Maspero was Director-General of the Department of Antiquities in Egypt.

◁▶ 15 drunken French visitors arrived at the excavations and demanded entry to the Necropolis. The ticket inspector demanded they pay – only 11 agreed.

◁▶ The guide accompanied them but asked to see each ticket before he'd unlock the door. The French ignored the request and forced open the door.

◁▶ It was dark inside. The visitors ordered the site foreman to bring them candles. He said he didn't have any. The French roughed him up and claimed their money back.

◁▶ The Egyptian inspector was called – they knocked his hat off and trampled it. While Carter was sent for the French tried to get their money back by force. Carter gave the order to eject the drunken French visitors. And that was what caused all the problems.

The French version painted a different set of hieroglyphs when their local newspaper ranted …

> 'The French party asked Carter why they should not have their money refunded. He replied very discourteously. He then ordered the guards to eject the party. A bloody fracas followed in which large stones were thrown. Finally the wounded were picked up and the whole party with difficulty retreated to safety'
>
> *Report in* L'Egypte *newspaper*

Carter defended the actions of his men and refused to apologise – he wouldn't acknowledge he'd done anything wrong. He was reassigned to a less sensitive job away from Cairo. Instead he resigned.

He spent the next few years in the archaeological wilderness, trying to make a living from selling his watercolours of Egyptian scenes. It was a hand-to-mouth existence. But he developed a sideline that would allow him luxuries like living in good hotels. He discreetly sold antiquities under the counter to help him stay afloat. They all did it at some time.

> 'There are a lot of perks that come with fame, and with every positive there's a negative, and then it all kind of balances out.'
>
> *Ashton Kutcher (1978—), American actor*

He didn't take antiquities to the local bazaar – or the Edwardian equivalent to a car boot sale. He was usually commissioned to 'obtain' those historic artefacts – take them from the Egyptian public and hand them over to the rich Western collectors. It was illegal and immoral, but a hungry man doesn't let those considerations stand in his way.

Carter needed contacts with the moneyed classes and his go-between was the wealthy aristocrat Lord Carnarvon.

It was Carnarvon who rescued Carter's career when, in 1909, he engaged him to dig at Thebes again. The dig was not a spectacular success. In the first season they found a mummified cat in a case.

World War I came along in 1914 and Carter's old intemperance led him to destroy the German archaeology headquarters.

Resourceful as ever, he bought up bargains in antiquities while the war disrupted the market, and became an agent for museums and private individuals. The Metropolitan Museum of Art in New York and other institutions were happy to enrich their Ancient Egyptian holdings, cashing in on the carnage and conflict that was causing the disorder.

After some disappointing excavations, Carnarvon decided to abandon his sponsorship of Carter's efforts. Carter persuaded him to have one last shot – one last throw of the dice on the game of snakes and ladders. They landed at the highest ladder of all when Carter uncovered the tomb of the Boy King.

The world was enriched by the finds ... mostly. The story they never tell you is that Carter probably pocketed a few trinkets as gifts to his supporters *before* the tomb was officially opened.

His career – his life – seems to have peaked there. The only way was down. He gave up excavating to become a collector. He also became somewhat lonely and despondent when the aftershocks of his discovery settled.

Once the work in the tomb had finished, he was to be seen pitiably seeking recognition in the lobby of Luxor's Winter Palace Hotel, like some Ancient Mariner hoping to trap a passing visitor into hearing (again) the tale of his moment in the golden glow of Tutankhamun's treasure, and the even brighter glow of fleeting fame.

> 'You don't understand. I coulda had class. I coulda been a contender. I coulda been somebody, instead of a bum, which is what I am, let's face it.'
>
> *Marlon Brando as 'Terry Malloy'*
> *in movie* On the Waterfront *(1954)*

His last years were marked by poor health and he died on 2 March 1939. Few mourners attended his burial. His grave was neglected for 60 years (until the British Museum finally remembered their debt to him).

Neglected in life, forgotten in death, rather like a lost mummified king. Maybe *that* was the real curse of Tutankhamun.

'May your spirit live, May you spend millions of years,
You who love Thebes,
Sitting with your face to the north wind,
Your eyes beholding happiness.
O night, spread thy wings over me as the
imperishable stars.'

Inscription on Howard Carter's restored headstone

— MARGARET MURRAY (1863–1963) —

'Many Egyptologists drew a distinction between
'Egyptomania', the fascination with all things Egypt,
and 'Egyptology', the scientific study of Egyptian life,
but Margaret Murray had a different goal – involving
the public in scientific inquiry with a goal of
correcting popular misconceptions.'

Science in Context journal, December 2012

A remarkable woman Egyptologist was Margaret Murray. She was tutored by Flinders Petrie and joined him on his excavations in Egypt. She went on to teach his classes while he went off on new expeditions. Flinders gave her a senior role and she came up against good old sexism as men grumbled about taking orders from a woman. The effect was to make Margaret a more ardent feminist.

Like Amelia Edwards before her she became a passionate supporter of the women's suffrage movement. She took part in the first large procession of the suffragette movement – The Mud March of 1907.*

---

* This was a traipse of 3,000 women through the muddy streets of London

But Margaret's studies in Egypt led her down some strange paths. She looked at Egyptian folklore and began to make connections with European legends. Her passion was the study of witchcraft.

She became president of the Folklore Society – they were thrilled to have a celebrity at their head. But some of her eccentric theories brought the Folklore Society into disrepute; like oddballs everywhere she could be an embarrassment. Someone should have told her.

> 'The reason to retire is to try to avoid embarrassment; you ought to do it before people are dropping big hints. You want to be the first to come up with the idea. You don't want to wait until you trip and fall off the stage.'
>
> *Garrison Keillor (1942—), American writer and humorist*

If you are of a nervous disposition you may not wish to read her theory that witches were members of a huge secret society preserving a prehistoric fertility cult and are still among us.

She not only wrote about witchcraft but practised it too. She was reported by friends to have cast spells in a saucepan to try to reverse academic appointments of which she disapproved.

At 96 she summed up her life ...

> 'I've been an archaeologist most of my life and now I'm a piece of archaeology myself.'
>
> *Margaret Murray, BBC Radio interview, 1959*

———

on a cold, wet February day. It was a first of its kind and an inspiration. By 1913 – the last mass march of the movement – there were 40,000 taking part and hundreds of thousands of spectators.

If her mentor Petrie argued that the Ancient Egyptians had been the product of European culture, then Murray argued that the whole of the modern world has been influenced by Egypt.

That is not quite as batty as Grafton Elliot Smith (1871–1937) who declared Egypt was the very start of civilisation. In this Nilotic Garden of Eden the first humans invented shaving, hats, pillows and wigs. But it was the invention of water pumps to irrigate the crops by the Nile that really changed the world. The man who invented the water pump (Grafton Elliot Smith wanted the world to believe) should be revered as a god, and honoured as Osiris after he died.

Now you know the secret of life. God is a hydraulic engineer.

— THE CURSES OF —
THE MUMMIES

Which is true?

> 'Superstition is the religion of feeble minds.'
> *Edmund Burke (1729–97), Irish statesman, philosopher*

Or …

> 'Superstition is the poetry of life.'
> *Johann Wolfgang von Goethe (1749–1832), German poet*

Answer? Both.

Superstition is mindless when people believe in nonsense and act upon it. When they believe in witchcraft then torture, hang and burn innocents.

Superstition is fun when we can suspend disbelief for a while and enjoy a tale of vampires or werewolves or dragons.*

Curses are superstitions that many believe quite irrationally. And the curses of the mummies are some of the tastiest tales to flavour our literature, movies and media.†

The basic fallacy is that the scripts the mummies were buried with are curses. Most are not. The Book of the Dead contains prayers, not curses. Only someone like Shakespeare would write a poetic plea to grave-robbers, skeleton-seekers and the corpse-curious.

> 'Good friend for Iesus sake forbeare,
> To digg the dust encloased heare.
> Blese be the man that spares thes stones,
> And cursed be he that moves my bones.'
>
> *Epitaph of William Shakespeare*

But if you do agree with Goethe that superstition is the poetry of life you will enjoy some of the mummy curse tales. Tales like …

Curse Tale 1

Akhenaten had changed the religion of his country to suit himself. He was despised after his death, rather like Richard III in England; centuries later, stories were told that discredited him.

---

* Or suspend our disbelief long enough to believe politicians will do what they promise in their manifesto. We know it's a fairy-tale that neither side believes.

† The first ghost story about a mummy's curse was published in 1699. Not a lot of people know that.

Akhenaten's religion may have changed but his belief in the afterlife hadn't. An especially nasty tale concerned one of his daughters. Only a complete body could pass into the afterlife. A report said that Akhenaten argued with one of his daughters and condemned her to be executed. But he had no wish to meet her in the afterlife so he had a hand cut off from her body.

The body was mummified and buried but the hand was left outside the coffin. It was passed through generations of an Egyptian family.*

There is a story that the mummified hand was taken to England in the 1920s – it was fashionable to have Egyptian relics decorating the mantelpieces of the middle classes – and the princess's ghost haunted the hand's owners. Are you sitting comfortably?

Count Louis Hamon was renowned as a psychic healer. On a visit to Egypt in 1890, Hamon cured a sheikh of malaria and the grateful man gave Hamon the mummified hand of an Egyptian princess.

Count Hamon's wife found the dry hand distasteful, more so when she heard the story of the murdered princess behind it.

Hamon locked the hand in an empty safe in the wall of his London home.

In October 1922, he opened the safe and was horrified to see the hand had changed – after 3,000 years a mummy it was now soft flesh again.

---

* Some might say it was handed down ... but I couldn't possibly inflict such a bad joke on you, dear reader.

Hamon's wife wanted it destroyed but Hamon thought it more proper to give it a decent cremation. On the night of 31 October 1922 Hamon laid the hand gently in the fireplace and read aloud a passage from the Egyptian Book of the Dead.*

As he closed the book there was a lightning strike that plunged the house into darkness. The door was blown open by a sudden chill wind and the couple were thrown to the floor. Looking up, they saw the ghostly and ghastly form of a woman. She was wearing the royal clothes of old Egypt and her right arm ended in a stump. The ghost bent over the fire and then vanished. The hand had disappeared with her.

Four days later, Hamon learned that his friend Lord Carnarvon had discovered Tutankhamun's tomb. Hamon sent his old friend a letter, asking him to think twice before opening the tomb. He wrote: 'I know now that the Ancient Egyptians had powers which we do not understand. In the name of God, I ask you to take care.'

Carnarvon never received the letter. He entered the Tut tomb and died soon after from a mosquito bite.

The ancient powers which we do not understand had led him to his doom.

All the members of Carnarvon's expedition died soon afterwards, killed by the Curse of the Pharaohs.†

---

* Details like the exact date always lend plausibility to a tall tale.
† Except they didn't. But the Curse of Tutankhamen is another story.

Curse Tale 2

'And the Lord God said unto the serpent, "Because thou hast done this, thou art cursed; upon thy belly shalt thou go, and dust shalt thou eat all the days of thy life."

Genesis 3:14

In the 1880s four Egyptian robbers dug up a mummy and took it away to sell. Each man was struck by a disaster – murdered, bankrupted, plagued by illness or simply vanished.

The mummy fell into the hands of a British Egyptologist who bought the mummy and returned with it to England. When his three sons were hurt in an accident and his house caught fire he sent it to the British Museum in London.

Even as it was delivered, there was a fearful accident ... the delivery driver's horse reared and sent the cart backwards. It crushed a man against a wall. As the mummy was carried up the museum stairs the stone coffin slipped, one man broke his leg. He went home quite healthy but two days later his wife called at the museum ... he'd died suddenly in the night.

When the museum opened the coffin and examined the mummy it was revealed that in life she had been the priestess Amun-Ra. A wicked woman who had a hundred people sold as slaves or tortured to death. Then in around 1500 BC one of her lovers stabbed her. As she lay dying, she used her powers to curse all men who came into contact with her corpse.

In the museum a cleaner tried to dust her coffin ... the cleaner's child died of measles the next day. A newspaper heard the stories and sent a photographer. The photo showed a face so hideous the man shot himself. So when the museum had an offer from America for this mummy they decided to sell her.

The coffin of Amun-Ra was loaded onto a ship, hidden in the captain's cabin. So Amun-Ra set off on her last journey. A journey across the Atlantic in April 1912. But she never reached America.

The ship was called RMS *Titanic*.

Curse tale 3

The most widely believed curse is, of course, that of Tutankhamun ...

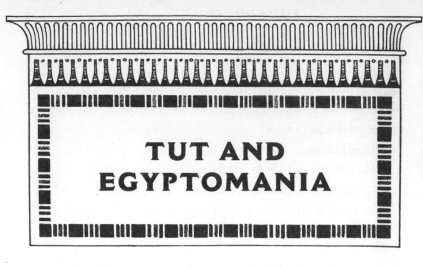

TUT AND EGYPTOMANIA

'He got into his royal bed,
Three thousand years BC.
And left a call for twelve o'clock
In nineteen twenty-three.'*

Lyrics 'Old King Tut Was a Wise Old Nut' by Roger Lewis (1923)†

The history of Tutankhamun as a pharaoh was short and none too sweet.

King Tutankhamun inherited the throne from his father Akhenaten – the odd pharaoh who worshipped the sun god Aten. Young Tutankhamun married his half-sister Ankhesenamun – the daughter of Queen Nefertiti – to secure his right to the throne.

---

* 'Three thousand years BC' scans better than 'thirteen-twenty-three BC' so forget the inaccuracy. And Carter found the tomb in 1922 but that doesn't rhyme with BC. The song, in line with Flinders Petrie's racism, suggested a black Egyptian pharaoh would have been unacceptable in 1920s America: 'Old King Tut was a wise old nut, with the pyramids on top; He had a show there ev'ry night no Ku Klux Klan could stop.'

† When the song was written Tut's coffin hadn't been opened. The lyricist didn't realise he was 'Young' King Tut.

And it needed securing. His father's fanatical devotion to the sun god had filled Egypt with rumbles of rebellion. The young heir was guided by his crafty old Uncle Ay and the experienced general Horemheb. The accession was assured – long life was not.

Tutankhamun died in January 1323 BC and the chief beneficiary was Uncle Ay. Had he backed young Tutankhamun as a puppet then decided to take the crown for himself? Not many people in history have agreed with the sainted US president who said …

> 'I would rather be a little nobody, than to be an evil somebody.'
>
> *Abraham Lincoln (1809–65), 16th US president*

A 20th-century X-ray analysis of Tutankhamun's mummy revealed that the young king may have died from a blow to the back of his head.

The suggestion still causes Egyptologists and scientists to squabble. Whodunnit? Was it Ay, Tutankhamun's geriatric vizier and uncle, who ascended to the throne after his death and married Tut's young wife, Ankhesenamun?

Or was it Horemheb, the army officer who became king after Ay's short four-year rule? Some experts say it was a team effort of the twosome.

Their X-ray analysis suggests that Tutankhamun may have been murdered in his sleep.

> 'The blow was to a protected area at the back of the head which you don't injure in an accident, someone had to sneak up from behind.'
>
> *US trauma specialist at Long Island University, USA*

It's possible (the experts say) that he lingered, maybe for as long as two months, before he died.

But the Director-General of the Egyptian Museum claims the boy king died of lung disease or even a brain tumour. 'This would explain the lump found on the back of his head,' he said.

Recent scans show he had malaria and circulation problems. It's amazing he lasted as long as he did. Who needs assassins when the king was as damaged as a crash-test dummy?

The funeral was arranged as hastily as a shotgun wedding. A non-royal tomb in the Valley of the Kings was appropriated.* Funeral trappings were borrowed from elsewhere. Tut's sarcophagus was second-hand ... a new granite lid was stuck on the quartzite base like some cowboy builder's bodge.

Yet perversely the very fact that a commoner's grave was usurped meant it was preserved for thousands of years.

Yes, the tomb of Tutankhamun *was* robbed soon after the funeral, but it was re-sealed with most of the treasures intact. Then the construction of another royal grave hid the entrance to Tut's tunnel under discarded spoil. So his mummy was left to rest in peace. But what about his spirit – his ka? Was it restless because the king died too soon and unavenged? Was Ay or Horemheb a killer?

If it was murder, let's not forget Tutankhamun's wife, Ankhesenamun, was in the frame. No sooner was hubby dead than she was contacting a Syrian monarch, asking him to send one of his sons to marry her following the death of her husband.

---

* Imagine the indignity of that? You've had a cosy tomb dug through rock and paid the undertakers good money. Just as you are resting in the knowledge your trip to Egyptian heaven is bought and paid for, along comes some royal bully and commandeers it. You'd be upset – but not spinning in your grave.

> 'Thrift, thrift, Horatio! The funeral baked meats
> Did coldly furnish forth the marriage tables.'
>
> *William Shakespeare:* Hamlet

There is even a theory that Tut was murdered by poison. Was she in league with his cup-bearer?

Agatha Christie, wife of an archaeologist, really ought to have put Poirot on the case.

— ANKHESENAMUN THE WIDOW —

> 'Can anyone understand how it is to have lived in the White House and then, suddenly, to be living alone as the President's widow?'
>
> *Jackie Kennedy (1929–94), widow of US president John Kennedy*

Ankhesenamun had been about eight years old when she married nine-year-old Tutankhamun. There was real affection it seemed. If tomb inscriptions are to be believed, they enjoyed one another's company – Ankhesenamun passed arrows to Tutankhamun when he went hunting and he, in turn, filled her hands with wine when she was thirsty. She doesn't look like a murderous wife in the tomb pictures.

We can guess they were well matched and happy ... but tragedy cast a long shadow over the happy couple before Tutankhamun died. Two babies were miscarried.

The unlucky young woman didn't have long to mourn her husband and half-brother. She was married to her grandfather. On the plus side, he was so old the marriage was blessedly short. But we can't state that she lived happy ever after as she disappears from history. She's forgotten like a discarded puppet. Someone else had always pulled the strings.

⏤ THAT QUAINT CURSE ⏤

Whatever happened to him, Tutankhamun was dead.

His tomb, in comparison with those of his predecessors, was modest.* (Maybe a clue to Ay's complicity in the death is that, after the boy-king's death, his successors tried to expunge Ay's memory by removing his name from all the official records. Even those carved in stone. Ironically, his enemy's efforts only ensured his eventual fame.)

Tut's tomb was then carefully sealed.

Egypt's best project planners designed the rock cave graves to resist thieves. In some cases heavy, hard-granite plugs were used to block passageways. In others, false doors and hidden rooms were designed to fool the felonious. Finally, in a few cases, a curse was placed on the entrance.

There *are* some examples of tomb curses … but no proof that they ever led to the misery of a mummy-mugger.

> 'As for anybody who shall enter this tomb in his impurity: I shall wring his neck as a bird's.'
>
> 'As for any man who shall destroy these, it is the god Thoth who shall destroy him.'
>
> 'As for him who shall destroy this inscription: He shall not reach his home. He shall not embrace his children. He shall not see success.'

---

* Well, if you've murdered your nephew for his power and wealth you're not going to bother putting too much of that wealth underground, are you? Ay, you're not.

These precautions failed. In ancient times grave-robbers found their way into the tombs. They hacked away door seals, chiselled their way around the plugs and discovered the secrets of the hidden doors. They stripped the dead pharaohs of their valuables.

In 1891 Howard Carter arrived in Egypt and found the graves had all been entered and robbed. But he became convinced that there was still one undiscovered tomb. That of the forgotten King Tutankhamun. Carter and his backer Lord Carnarvon searched for five years but found nothing.

Carnarvon began to have doubts and summoned Carter to England in 1922 to tell him he was abandoning the search. On his return to Egypt, the archaeologist brought with him a yellow canary.

'A golden bird!' Carter's Egyptian foreman, Reis Ahmed, exclaimed. 'It will lead us to the gold of the tomb.' Maybe it did. On 4 November 1922 Howard Carter discovered a step cut into a rock that had been hidden by debris left over from the building of the tomb of Ramesses IV.

At least, that's what the world believes. The truth is a native Egyptian water boy scooped a hollow in the earth so his water jars wouldn't fall over. He accidentally uncovered the first step to the tunnel that led to Tutankhamun's tomb. Carter got the fame and fortune that went with the water boy's discovery.

> 'A journey of a thousand miles begins with a single step.'
> *Lao-tzu (604–531 BC), Chinese philosopher*

In Carter's case, the journey of a thousand artefacts started with that single step. They found 15 more steps leading to an ancient door with an unbroken seal. On the door was the name 'Tutankhamun'.

The legends say that when Carter arrived home that night his servant met him at the door. He opened his hand to reveal a few yellow feathers. The servant babbled that the canary had been killed by a cobra. Carter merely told the servant to make sure the snake was out of the house.

The trembling man grabbed Carter by the sleeve. 'The pharaoh's serpent ate the bird because it led us to the hidden tomb. You must not disturb the grave.'

Carter dismissed it as superstitious nonsense and sent the man home. He had more important things on his mind than a canary that had chirped its last. He had to send a telegram to Carnarvon in England.

> 'At last have made wonderful discovery in Valley; a magnificent tomb with seals intact, re-covered same for your arrival; congratulations.'

Out of courtesy he wanted his paymaster to be there at the kill … as it were. He may as well have invited Carnarvon to his own funeral.*

Carnarvon arrived in Egypt in November and watched as Carter made a hole in the door. Carter leaned in, holding a candle, to take a look.

Carter's own account says …

> 'As my eyes grew accustomed to the light, details of the room within emerged slowly from the mist, strange animals, statues, and gold – everywhere the glint of gold. For the moment – an eternity it must have seemed to the others standing by – I was struck

---

* Over the top? Melodramatic? All right. But the fact remains, if Carnarvon had stayed in England he may have lived to pick up his pension.

> dumb with amazement, and when Lord Carnarvon, unable to stand the suspense any longer, inquired anxiously, "Can you see anything?" it was all I could do to get out the words, "Yes, wonderful things."'*
>
> *Howard Carter:* Tomb of Tutankhamun

The day the tomb was opened was one of joy and celebration for all those involved. Nobody seemed to be concerned about any curse.

— THE CARNARVON CUT —

> 'Along the valley of the Nile, tonight a torch is flamin' Because two excavators found the tomb of Tut Ankh Hamen.'
>
> *'Old King Tut Was a Wise Old Nut'*, Roger Lewis

Tutankhamun's tomb was mostly intact, though two of the chambers had been ransacked soon after the burial and hastily repacked by Necropolis guards. The other chambers contained an amazing collection of treasures, including a stone sarcophagus. The sarcophagus contained three gold coffins nested within each other. Inside the final one was the mummy of the boy-king, Pharaoh Tutankhamun.

The public was gripped. Newspapers profited. Celebrities offered opinions. Marie Corelli wrote ...

---

* There are some historians who believe Carter invented this iconic answer much later – when Carnarvon was too dead to contradict him. His actual answer may have been more along the lines of, 'I'm so excited I could crush a grape.'

'I cannot but think some risks are run by breaking into the last rest of a king in Egypt whose tomb is specially and solemnly guarded, and robbing him of his possessions. According to a rare book I possess . . . entitled *The Egyptian History of the Pyramids* (an ancient Arabic text), the most dire punishment follows any rash intruder into a sealed tomb. The book names "secret poisons enclosed in boxes in such wise that those who touch them shall not know how they come to suffer". That is why I ask, Was it a mosquito bite that has so seriously infected Lord Carnarvon?'

Marie Corelli (1855–1924), British novelist, letter to New York and London newspapers *

Ms Corelli – ever the sensational novelist – started the rumour of a specific Tut curse with a description of a carved inscription of doom. This alleged curse read ...

'Death Shall Come on Swift Wings To Him Who Disturbs the Peace of the King.' †

Later rumours said that Carter had found a tablet with this curse inscribed on it, but hid it so it would not scare his workers. Carter denied any such inscription existed. Then again, he would.

---

* Marie *who*? you ask. Astonishingly, from 1886 until World War I, Corelli's novels sold more copies than the combined sales of three of her contemporaries: Arthur Conan Doyle, H. G. Wells and Rudyard Kipling.
† Even today, it is easy to find books that report this inscription as fact. This is simply not true. Luckily you are reading a Dangerous Days book that is honest as the day is long ... your honour.

There is no doubt what happened next. A few months after the tomb's opening, Lord Carnarvon, aged 57, was taken ill and rushed to Cairo. He died a few days later. Death seems to have come from a shaving cut on a healing mosquito bite. It became infected and the infection killed him.* Fact.

Legend? Legend has it that when he died there was a power failure and all the lights throughout Cairo went out. His son reported that back on his estate in England his favourite dog howled and suddenly dropped dead.

Legend says that when the mummy of Tutankhamun was unwrapped in 1925, it was found to have a wound on the left cheek in the exact same position as the insect bite on Carnarvon that led to his death.

Legend says that by 1929, 11 people connected with the discovery of the Tomb had died early and of unnatural causes. This included two of Carnarvon's relatives, Carter's personal secretary, Richard Bethell, and Bethell's father, Lord Westbury. Westbury killed himself by jumping from a building. He left a note that read,

> 'I really cannot stand any more horrors and hardly see what good I am going to do here, so I am making my exit.'

What horrors did Westbury refer to? His son, Richard Bethell, was found smothered to death at a Mayfair club.

The press followed the deaths and by 1935 they had attributed 21 victims to Tutankhamun's curse.

---

* Perhaps he should have used 'Reade Brother's Egyptian Salve – good for sores, wounds, ulcers, abscesses, burns, eruptions and skin diseases.' It had no connection to Egypt but was part of the Egyptomania business.

— LEGENDS AND LIES —

> 'He did not himself believe in the supernatural, but the thing happened, and he proposed to tell it as simply as possible.'
>
> *T.H. White** (1906–64), English author:*
> *Ghostly, Grim and Gruesome*

Come up with a miracle and someone will try to explain it. 'He walked on water? Nah, he was water-skiing.'

Herbert E. Winlock (1884–1950) was a New York Egyptologist and was the wet blanket when it came to studying the effectiveness of the curse. He said there were 26 people present when the tomb was opened in 1922 and only 6 had died by 1934.

Of the 22 people present at the opening of the coffin in 1924, only 2 died in the following 10 years.

Of the 10 people who were there when the mummy was unwrapped in 1925, all survived until at least 1934.

EVENT	NUMBER OF PEOPLE PRESENT	NUMBER DEAD AFTER 10 YEARS
Burial chamber opening (1922)	26	6
Sarcophagus opening (1924)	22	2
Mummy unwrapping (1925)	10	0

Curse-mongers still argue, 'Ah, but those people exposed to the curse died at an average age of 70. The Europeans in

---

* Author of the sequence of Arthurian novels, *The Once and Future King.* King Arthur – another legend that defies common sense and historical evidence. People just *want* to believe, so they do. Funny things, people.

Egypt at the same time have lived to an average age of 75. See? It's the curse.'

You have to smile and walk away ... cursing.*

> 'The curse is simply nonsense and dangerous because it goes to swell the rising tide of superstition which at present seems to be overflowing the world.'
>
> *Sir Henry Rider Haggard*

Other lies have been exposed down the years ... Carter's canary was never eaten by a snake but given to a friend named Minnie Burton to care for and she gave it (alive and well) to a bank manager.

As for the lights going out all over Cairo at Lord Carnarvon's death, power failures in Cairo in 1923 were a common occurrence and a supernatural cause is hardly needed to explain them.

The dead dog in England? No proof either way.

Even Carnarvon's death seems unsurprising as he was already in poor health before the opening of the tomb. Infections, in the days before the invention of antibiotics, were a common cause of death.

Sir Arthur Conan Doyle suggested that Egyptian priests may have placed spores in King Tut's tomb to punish grave robbers. This wacky theory has been backed up by a modern scientist who said anthrax spores can survive for centuries.

No one has explained how the priests gathered these spores and seeded the tomb in the days before face-masks had been invented. There should have been a train of clerical corpses on the path to the king's contaminated coffin.

---

* Or you could say, 'Everyone at Queen Victoria's funeral is now dead. It was cursed too, you know.'

If not a 'curse', could a fungal infection have been to blame – sick-making spores that were stirred up when air entered the tomb? Sorry, none of the victims died of a fungal infection.

> 'Given the sanitary conditions of the time in general, and those within Egypt in particular, Lord Carnarvon would likely have been safer inside the tomb than outside.'
>
> *F. DeWolfe Miller, professor of epidemiology*

And the final nail in the mystic mumbo-jumbo? Howard Carter, the man who actually opened the tomb, never believed in the curse and lived to a reasonably old age of 64 before dying of entirely natural causes.

— THE TEACHING FROM TUT —

> 'A Conspiracy!' cried the delighted lady, clapping her hands. 'Of all things, I do like a Conspiracy! It's so interesting!'
>
> *Lewis Carroll (1832–98), English writer and mathematician*

Tutankhamun's tomb gave us useful clues on the subject of tomb-robbing. The ancient burial party kept inventories of everything that had been included in Tutankhamun's grave goods. That written record was buried with the king, so we can work out which objects were missing from the original funerary collection.

But it also tells us about the kind of things the thieves were after.

It seems most robbers went first for precious metals that could easily be melted down.

The perishable goods – the expensive oils, spices and wine – were usually removed during the first wave of pilfering.

Next on the robber's shopping list came the rich linens and clothing.

A lot of funerary decoration was stolen before the tomb was even sealed. (We can picture an Egyptian priest with a gold statue shoved down his loincloth perhaps?)

The tomb of Tutankhamun *was* robbed twice shortly after his funeral.

'As we cleared the passage we found mixed with the rubble broken potsherds, jar seals, and numerous fragments of small objects; water skins lying on the floor together with alabaster jars, whole and broken, and coloured pottery vases; all pertaining to some disturbed burial, but telling us nothing to whom they belonged further than by their type which was of the late 18th Dynasty. These were disturbing elements as they pointed towards plundering.'

Howard Carter: The Discovery of the Tomb of Tutankhamun (1933)

How had robbers beaten the defences? The tunnel into the tomb had been sealed with tons of limestone chips. The robbers made a narrow tunnel through the chippings and broke in on two occasions. A scarf, twisted round 30 precious rings, was found in the passageway that the robbers used. They must have been in such a hurry to get away they dropped part of the loot.

They may have tried to steal some of the golden furniture, thinking they could melt it down. When they found it was just wooden furniture covered in gold leaf, they threw it back into the tomb.

We do not know if the ring-robbers were caught or if they escaped. The punishment for tomb-robbers was to have the soles of their feet beaten with rods before being impaled on a sharp stick until death released them from their agony.

Robbers' rules

> 'When morality comes up against profit, it is seldom that profit loses.'
>
> *Shirley Chisholm (1924–2005), US politician and author*

Tutankhamun's grave had been forgotten. The other pharaohs' graves were not. A special Arabic handbook for tomb-robbers called *The Book of Burial Pearls*, written around 1450, gave details of buried treasure and tips for sneaking past the spirits that guarded the dead.

If the kings were preserved for the afterlife then the robbers wrecked the royal plans. Why would Egyptians wilfully desecrate the grave of their pharaoh and cause him eternal misery? How would the robbers defend their thievery?

They would probably say that high taxes were levied on the peasants to pay for offerings to the royal dead. It was a fair deal for us peasants – you pay to keep the dead god-king happy and he makes sure your life on earth is comfortable.

But when plagues and storms, famines and riots struck, then that old mummy was not keeping up his end of the deal. Rob him. Get back what he owes you. It's not robbery ... is it? You could even argue that robbing a tomb of its treasures put cash back into the economy. Today we call it quantitative easing and think it's a 21st-century invention.* But the Egyptian villains got there first with that idea, it seems.

> 'What has been is what will be, and what has been done is what will be done, and there is nothing new under the sun.'
>
> *Ecclesiastes 1:9*

— TUT-MANIA —

> 'Most people seek after what they do not possess and are enslaved by the very things they want to acquire.'
>
> *Anwar Sadat (1918–81), Egyptian president*†

If people are interested in Ancient Egypt today it's usually not because of the dusty schoolbooks and dustier history teachers. It's because of the public infatuation with young Tutankhamun which began when his grave was uncovered. The love affair has hardly diminished since.

---

* Quantitative easing is a 21st-century term for an ancient idea. It was revived in 2000 AD in Japan. The Japanese banks were saying it wouldn't work. So what did the Western economies do in 2008? Yes, they copied it. Egyptian robbers were probably better economists than the banks that rob.
† Such wisdom is admirable. Some of his other thoughts are not. This ex-army officer never lost his military pugnacity and contempt for civilians, as when he said, 'The best way to deal with bureaucrats is with stealth and sudden violence.'

TEN THINGS YOU SHOULD KNOW ABOUT TUT-MANIA

1 The first bout of Tut-mania swept through the 1920s. It expressed itself through fashion and fads, and even had a more permanent effect on architecture. Ancient Egyptian-style clothes quickly hit the markets and appeared in fashion magazines.

2 Daily updates of the find were demanded. Masses of mail and telegrams swamped Carter and his colleagues. Reporters followed Carter around as if he was a film star.*

3 Hundreds of tourists waited outside the tomb for a glimpse. Hundreds more tried to use their influential friends to get a tour of the tomb, hindering work in the tomb and risking damage to the finds.

4 Tut-mania gave rise to a whole new art movement. Can you guess what it is? It took its name from an exhibit of Egyptian-inspired art objects in Paris that was called 'Les Arts Décoratifs d'Egypte.' Guessed it yet? The movement came to be called 'Art Deco'.

5 Tut-mania coincided with the birth of the great movie palaces. Hence many cinemas from that time were designed to look like Egyptian temples.

---

* Rival (and jealous) archaeologists said that Carter invented the curse to gain more fame and the press reporters adopted it religiously to make headlines. Poor Tut was exploited in life and then when he was dead.

6 In the 1920s you could dance to the 'Tutankhamun Rag' played by a jazz orchestra in the ballroom of the Winter Palace Hotel, Luxor.

7 In the early 1970s Richard Nixon made a triumphal state visit to Egypt in the fading days of his doomed presidency. He was looking for something – anything – that could be hailed as an 'agreement' to take home. Nixon and Egyptian president Anwar Sadat reached agreement on a travelling exhibition of Tut's funerary haul. By 1976, some 55 of the choicest artefacts were crossing the Atlantic. It didn't save Nixon.

8 The 1978 'Treasures of Tutankhamun' exhibition saw some eight million visitors at the Metropolitan Museum of Art — not only more than the population of New York at the time, but more than the entire population of Egypt that Tut ruled when he was alive.

9 The young pharaoh, who was obscure during his own reign, had been forgotten. Now he has become one of the best-known pharaohs of Ancient Egypt. Having toured around the world as part of an exhibition, King Tut's body again rests in his tomb in the Valley of the Kings.

10 In the 21st century the Tut artefacts rarely leave Egypt. A major exhibition continues to tour the world, but everything in it is a replica. It still attracts queues around the block ... or the pyramid. It's as if the King Tut Tribute Band is playing at the Albert Hall.

The lyrics and the losers

Tutankhamun and his treasures were adopted by the world.

The world also exploited Tut-mania. Dozens of songs were written to cash in on sheet-music sales. The whole family could gather round the piano and sing along to …

- 'That Quaint Egyptian Glide' which includes words your spellchecker will accept: 'Roll your eyes and every thing like a real Egyptianese. Oh!'

- 'Rose of Egyptland' – another new word.

- 'Ilo: a Voice from Mummy Land' – and another name for Egypt with the geographically inept line, 'I'm on my way again to Madagascar.' Uh?

- 'My Sahara Rose' is just as geographically challenged: 'I saw her face, / 'twas in the market place / of old Baghdad.'

- 'Cleopatra Had a Jazz Band' has the interesting (though historically unverified) lines: 'Caesar came from Rome to learn to dance the latest step, / And when he heard those Jazzers play he sure was full of pep.'

- 'Mummy Mine'* is a romantic song with ghoulish lyrics like, 'With your shrouded hands hold me.' Yeuch.

- 'The Mummies Ball'. Feel free to write your own witty rejoinder to that title. The song included the tragic 'Old King Ramesses shook himself to pieces, / Dancing at the mummies ball.'

---

* No that's not a song about a mine where you dig for mummies. And the opening, 'Mummy, a million years you have been sleeping, friendlessly' would get you a fail mark in a history exam. Five thousand years just doesn't scan so well.

'My Egyptian Mummy' is not much better: 'My Egyptian mummy, we were sweethearts years ago, that's why I know, though you were turned to stone, I almost hear you moan, I'm in love with you.' A song about reincarnation then.

'My Cleopatra' with timeless rhymes like, 'My Cleopatra! / I ain't no flatt'rer, / but dis is true; / if you don't want me, / Why will you haunt me, / de way you do?'

'My Egypt Maid' featuring the bizarre verse: 'One night to the land of the wondrous Sphinx / There came a man from o'er the hill. / He saw this maid and cried 'Me thinks / She's just the girl I'm looking for / To get a booking for in vaudeville.'

Exploiting Egypt

Egyptomania meant money. Links with Egypt were seen as an endorsement for more than mere music.

Lord Carnarvon himself cashed in when he sold his exclusive story to *The Times* for £5,000, a practice that was almost unheard of in those days. He didn't live to enjoy it, of course.

London Underground jumped on the bandwagon with witty advertisements like, 'Yes, it is odd, living in the tomb of Tutankhamun… but we thought the agent said a room in Tooting Common.'

Tobacco manufacturing became a major Egyptian industry and European cigar and ciggie makers used Egyptian imagery to sell their dangerous smokes. 'Royal Queen' cigarettes featured an image of Cleopatra adapted from a popular painting of the day. Knowing as we now do the dangers of tobacco, the title of that painting is the ultimate irony; it is called ...

> 'Cleopatra Testing Poisons on Condemned Prisoners'

☥ Merchants in Cairo's Khan el-Khalili Bazaar were selling Touth-Ankh-Amon perfume to tourists. In the US you could enjoy 'King Tut Cologne'. Yes, you too could smell like someone who's been dead a few thousand years.

☥ Silent movies began depicting Egyptian tales, like *Cleopatra* starring Theda Bara* as Egypt's femme fatale. She was a Jewish American but for $4,000 a week she'd act her socks off to play a Greek Egyptian.

☥ A series of mummy movies in the US and UK exploited the Egyptomania craze. In America Ramesses III was played by Tom Tyler, who was crippled by arthritis; his stiff movement was (unfortunately) accurate for an embalmed man who'd been entombed for 3,000 years. In the UK the mummy was played by Christopher Lee – and those were dangerous days for the bandaged actor. His character had to barge through a door; a stage-manager left the door locked so Christopher dislocated his shoulder. The mummy films were

---

* Real name a less exotic Theodosia Burr Goodman, daughter of Cincinnati tailor Bernard. Her stage name is an anagram of Arab Death and her nickname 'The Vamp', short for Vampire. Her publicists claimed that she was 'the daughter of an Arab sheikh and a French woman', born 'in the shadow of the Sphinx'. Captivating. But an Arab sheikh named Bernard Goodman? No.

awful. Maybe the comic *Abbot and Costello Meet the Mummy* (1955) got it right. Charlton Heston's mummy film, *The Awakening*, was so bad it closed within a week of its release.

👁 Cleopatra was treated more glamorously in movies than the mummy, but almost as inaccurately. The Elizabeth Taylor version (1963) had a budget of $5 million. The cursed production had so many problems it overspent by nearly $40 million. Egyptomania wasn't always profitable.

But the saddest losers are probably the Egyptian people. The Egyptomanic world took the country's treasures and left a reasonable tourist industry. Not quite a fair exchange.

EPILOGUE

'The past is never dead. It's not even past.'

William Faulkner (1897–1962), American writer

Wiliam Faulkner won a Nobel Prize for saying clever things like that. He meant that we are all linked to the past. (I think that's what he meant. Maybe.)

Mr Faulkner may have had Ancient Egypt in mind when he wrote that. After all, there are museums stuffed with treasures of the pharaohs, there are buildings inspired by Egyptian designs (like the Art Deco influence on the Empire State Building in New York City), there are movies inspired by mummies as well as homes filled with Art Deco furniture, fabrics and fireplaces.

A civilisation that died 2,000 years ago isn't dead. Isn't past.

'But truth itself is for eternity.'

'The Tale of the Eloquent Peasant': Egyptian text (1850 BC)

Life in Ancient Egypt was short – 40 was a good age to reach. So as the pages of the calendar sped by like dancing figures on a zoetrope, the ancient citizens must have thought, 'There *has* to be something more.' You couldn't lie on your deathbed, stare at the fading light and say, 'Is that it then? Is that all?'

What more could there be? Another life perhaps? An *after*life. And it had to be better than this harsh and unpredictable existence with fitful spells of happiness and misery.

The people at the top – the pharaohs – expected to maintain their status in that afterlife and the myths grew around their supernatural powers to carry on. The two key myths were that you had to be good in this life to pass through the gateway to eternal happiness – sins would cause your heart to tip the scales when it came to weighing it in the great balance.

And of course you had to keep your body intact. Mummification was essential. You couldn't enjoy the next world if your body was eaten by worms or crumbled to dust. Even missing a forefinger would be a nuisance – how would you summon a slave … or pick your spiritual nose?

In time, the pharaoh's subjects began to resent the privilege the powerful had, to be reborn in a better world. They decided heaven was a communist state and everyone could enter – rich or poor – so long as their body wasn't destroyed, of course.

For 2,000 years the Egyptian rich and poor shared the happy dream …

> 'My head pierced the sky, I grazed the body of the stars, I danced like the planets.'
>
> *Tomb inscription of Sarenput, Prince of Elephantine*

But that was the downfall of the longest-running empire in history. Once the pharaohs lost their unique key that opened the door to the afterlife, they lost their magic. They stopped being gods, they stopped being special. They lost the fear of the people. Eternity was open to paupers as well as princes, layabouts and ladies, fishermen and pharaohs.

Everyone could hope for a place in the western skies.

> 'In awe I watched the waxing moon ride across the zenith of the heavens like an ambered chariot towards the ebony void of infinite space wherein the tethered belts of Jupiter and Mars hang, forever festooned in their orbital majesty. And as I looked at all this I thought ... I must put a roof on this toilet.'
>
> *Les Dawson (1931–93), English comedian*

The mighty pharaohs had made a deal with the peasants. They said, 'Work to make my life and afterlife rich and I will care for you when I die.'

Eventually the peasants realised they weren't getting a very good deal. When new pretenders challenged the pharaohs, the people threw in their lot with the one who offered the best deal for them ... in *this* life. No respect for the godlike pharaoh. Just a challenge to him: 'What's in it for me?'

That's progress.

> 'The test of our progress is not whether we add more to the abundance of those who have much; it is whether we provide enough for those who have too little.'
>
> *Franklin D. Roosevelt (1882–1945), 32nd US president*

Ancient Egypt is not dead. The past is never past, as long as we remember it.

We can only measure ourselves against our ancestors if we understand the dangerous days they lived through. Once we answer the question, 'Why do people behave the way they do?' then we are an ell closer to answering the biggest question of all – the one that is bigger than a pyramid – 'Why do *I* behave the way *I* do?'

> 'If you would know yourself, take yourself as starting point and go back to its source; your beginning will disclose your end.'
>
> *Inscription in Temple of Luxor, Egypt*

THE END

INDEX

Out now
The first instalment in
the Dangerous Days series

'Infamy! Infamy! They've all got it in-for-me,' Julius Caesar cried as he fell under the thrusts of twenty daggers. Oh, all right, Caesar didn't cry that, Kenneth Williams did in the movie *Carry on Cleo*. But nor did he sigh 'Et tu, brute?' as Shakespeare would have us believe. The history we think we know is full of misconceptions, mischiefs, misunderstandings . . . and monks who misused their spell-checkers.

What the general reader needs is a history that explores our ancestors with humour and compassion. 'Humour' and 'history' are not words you often see in the same sentence: our past was a dangerous and dirty place full of cruel rulers, foul food and terrible toilets. A short life, not a merry one, for most. Dangerous days in which to live and, inevitably, die . . .

Find out more at www.orionbooks.co.uk

WEIDENFELD & NICOLSON

Out now
The second instalment in
the Dangerous Days series

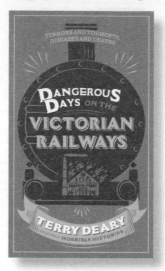

Facing feuds and frauds, robberies and riots and the disasters of dangerous drivers, deadly designers and sleepy signalmen, Victorians risked more than just delays when stepping on a steam train.

Victorian inventors certainly didn't lack steam, but squabbling over who deserved the title of 'The Father of the Locomotive' and busy enjoying their fame and fortune, safety on the rails was not their priority. Brakes were seen as a needless luxury (until a steamer started to slide downhill towards disaster) and boilers had an inconvenient tendency to overheat and explode, and in turn, blow up anyone in reach.

The victims of the Victorian railways had names, lives and families, and they deserve to be remembered . . .

Find out more at www.orionbooks.co.uk

Out now
The third instalment in
the Dangerous Days series

The reign of Elizabeth I – a Golden Age? Try asking her subjects . . .

Elizabethans did all they could to survive in an age of sin and bling, of beddings and beheadings, galleons and guns. Explorers set sail for new worlds, risking everything to bring back slaves, gold and the priceless potato. Elizabeth lined her coffers while her subjects lived in squalor with hunger, violence and misery as bedfellows.

Shakespeare shone and yet the beggars and thieves, the doxies and bawdy baskets, kinchins and fraters scraped and cheated to survive in the shadows. These were dangerous days. If you survived the villains, and the diseases didn't get you, then the lawmen might. Pick the wrong religion and the scaffold or stake awaited you. The toothless, red-wigged queen sparkled in her jewelled dresses, but the Golden Age was only the surface of the coin. The rest was base metal . . .

Find out more at www.orionbooks.co.uk

WEIDENFELD & NICOLSON